BAPTISM

BAPTISM

ITS PLACE AND IMPORTANCE IN CHRISTIANITY, WITH A LETTER CONCERNING HOUSEHOLD BAPTISM.

BY

PHILIP MAURO

WIPF & STOCK · Eugene, Oregon

Wipf and Stock Publishers
199 W 8th Ave, Suite 3
Eugene, OR 97401

Baptism
Its Place and Importance in Christianity, with a Letter Concerning Household Baptism
By Mauro, Philip
Copyright © 1914 by Mauro, Philip All rights reserved.
Softcover ISBN-13: 979-8-3852-4980-0
Hardcover ISBN-13: 979-8-3852-4981-7
eBook ISBN-13: 979-8-3852-4982-4
Publication date 3/25/2025
Previously published by Morgan and Scott, 1914

PREFACE

DURING a considerable time preceding the writing of these pages the subject of Baptism had been pressed upon my attention in various ways. Letters reached me from parts of the earth remote from each other, asking information as to the teaching of the Bible on that subject. Yielding to this pressure, and not with an inclination to do so [but rather the reverse], I turned to the Scriptures, seeking enlightenment from the fountain-head. I consulted no commentaries or treatises on the subject, nor had I previously given it any special study.

My main object was to learn just what importance was given to Baptism by the Lord Himself, seeing that there were, among Christians, so many different opinions about it.

The quest for light on this subject has proved to be exceedingly interesting and profitable, not merely in that it led to information upon the particular matter under consideration, but also, and chiefly, because it has resulted in a clearer apprehension of the entire truth of Redemption.

The results have been, in some respects, unexpected, not to say surprising; for it has been found that the Word of God closely links Baptism with the great foundation facts and truths of Christianity. This intimate connection is pointed out in the following pages.

Furthermore, while engaged upon the study of the general subject of Baptism, the special topic of "Household Baptism" was pressed upon my attention in the manner stated in the Introduction to Part II. of this Volume.

From these incidents it seems probable that my mind was divinely guided to the study of this great but much-neglected subject; and the results of the studies tend to confirm that belief.

Therefore, I feel warranted in urging my fellow-Christians to read these pages, and to meditate prayerfully upon the Scriptures referred to therein. It will surely be to their advantage to do so, for [whatever conclusions they may reach] it will at least serve to bring to their minds "those things which are most surely believed among us," and which lie at the foundation of our faith, hope, joy, and peace.

PHILIP MAURO.

Sturry, England,
March 25, 1914.

CONTENTS

Contents

PART II
HOUSEHOLD BAPTISM

PART I

BAPTISM: ITS PLACE AND IMPORTANCE

IN CHRISTIANITY

PART I

Its Place and Importance in Christianity

IN these days the subject of baptism is receiving little attention from those to whom many of the Lord's people look for their instruction in Divine things. Apparently the great majority of those who are not sacramentarians regard baptism as of little importance. As a natural consequence of this neglect of the **doctrine** of baptism, the **thing itself** is very largely neglected.

Furthermore, there is much conflict of opinion among teachers in regard to baptism. Among the disputed points are the significance of baptism, the mode of administering it, and persons who are its proper subjects. The existence of this conflict is, by many teachers, made an excuse for avoiding the whole subject. But it furnishes, on the contrary, a strong reason why every believer should settle the

3

matter for himself, upon his knees, seeking God's mind about it as expressed in the Bible.

It is not pleasant to engage in controversy. Nevertheless, the desire to avoid controverted subjects should not be permitted to control those who have responsibilities toward God and His people. If they would be, like Paul, "pure from the blood of all men," they must imitate him in not shunning "to declare all the counsel of God" (Acts xx. 26, 27).

Then we should inquire whether there be any valid excuse for the existing conflict about baptism. Baptism was included among the few and simple instructions which the Lord gave to His disciples on parting with them, and which were to be carried out by them in all nations of the world, and in all the days of this long age (Matt. xxviii. 19, 20). Did He then leave one of those important commandments in such obscurity that there is valid reason for differences of opinion about it? Such a thought could not be entertained for a moment. It cannot be that there is any lack of clearness in the Scriptures. The trouble must be in ourselves. And most likely it is in our hearts, rather than in our heads. There can be no doubt that such as **will** to do God's will in this matter, and who seek the knowledge of His will in order to do it, shall be given to know of the doctrine. Evidently there was no uncertainty about it at the beginning; for when Peter said, "Repent, and be baptized every one of you," there was no hesitation as to what should be done. For it is written that "then they that gladly **received his word** were baptized" (Acts ii. 38, 41).

The subject of baptism has lately been pressed upon the writer's attention in such a way as to impel him to search the Scriptures in the endeavour to ascertain for himself the mind of the Lord about it. One result of this study has been to convict him of slighting a matter which, in the light of God's Word, is of exceeding importance. This confession he feels bound to make. And furthermore, as an attempt to repair, if only in a slight degree, the consequences of this neglect, these pages are written for the eye of his fellow-Christians; not that they might accept his conclusions, but that they might search the Scriptures, each for himself, as the writer has done, to see whether these things be so.

One thing should be noted at the outset, namely, that the **practice** of baptism long preceded the unfolding of the **doctrine** of baptism. The spiritual significance of baptism was not explained until Paul's Epistles were written. Such being the case, it is evident that an understanding of the doctrine of baptism is not needed for the proper carrying out of the act. In fact, when confronted with a commandment of the Lord, it is best that we give our minds **first to the fulfilment of it,** and afterwards we may profitably inquire into its spiritual significance. The Bible is often studied for other purposes than to learn God's will with a view to doing it. There is a certain pleasure in merely acquiring knowledge of the Scriptures, and in displaying that knowledge to others. Against this tendency of our deceitful hearts, which seek in every direction for material to feed the natural pride of man, we need ever to be watchful. Furthermore, in some Christian companies a high value is placed upon extensive acquaintance with the doctrines of Scripture; and the ability to state these in accordance with approved theological formularies is regarded almost as the height of Christian attainment.

On the other hand, it is certain that what is pleasing in God's sight is, not a **head** well stocked with Biblical knowledge, but an obedient **heart,** a submissive **will,** and **feet** that are trained to walk in His holy ways.

It is likely that the Israelites did not comprehend the significance of circumcision, or the typical meaning of the offerings. But such lack of knowledge did not hinder them in following the directions given in the law.

So, in regard to baptism, those who set up a certain theory as to its **significance**, derived, it may be, by profound (though not necessarily spirit-guided) studies of Old Testament types, and then attempt to deduce from such theory conclusions as to the proper carrying out of the act of baptism, are likely to err.

The directions which the Lord gave to His disciples, and which the Spirit of God has caused to be recorded in the last chapters of Matthew and Mark respectively, were, and are, amply sufficient for the proper carrying out of the Lord's parting command. We should, of course, highly prize the explanations, subsequently given by inspiration of God, as to the spiritual significance of baptism. Nevertheless, those explanations are not necessary to the carrying out of the Lord's commandments. We should look, first of all, to **His words:** "For Moses truly said unto the fathers, A prophet shall the Lord your God raise up unto you of your brethren, like unto me; Him shall ye hear in all things whatsoever He shall say unto you. And it shall come to pass, that every soul, which will not hear that prophet, shall be destroyed from among the people" (Acts iii. 22, 23; cf. Deut. xviii. 15-22).

THE IMPORTANCE OF BAPTISM

Let us at the outset ascertain what is the importance of baptism in the Lord's own estimation. This may be learned by observing the place which He gave it in His last command to His followers. He charged them to make disciples out of **all** nations, baptizing them (the disciples) into the Name of the Father, and of the Son, and of the Holy Ghost. And in connection with this charge He gave the promise, "And lo, I am with you alway (all the days), even unto the end of the age" (Matt. xxviii. 19, 20). The command, then, is for **all the nations** of the world, and for **all the days** of the age. This fact testifies strongly to the great importance of baptism.

The importance of baptism also appears by its direct connection with the *NAME* (the one Name, not three names) of the Father, and of the Son, and of the Holy Spirit. We do not now pause to inquire what is meant by being baptized into this wondrous "Name"; for, whatever details may be involved, there can be no question that we have here a matter of the very highest importance. One who has been made a disciple of Christ is thereupon to be baptized into that **Divine Name which specially represents the Revelation of God in this dispensation of Grace.** Baptism brings him **into that Name.**

The importance of baptism appears further in the Lord's words recorded in Mark xvi. 15, 16: "And He said unto them, Go ye into all the world, and preach the Gospel to every creature (to the entire creation). He that **believeth** and is **baptized** shall be **saved**; but he that believeth not (**dis**believes) shall be damned (condemned)."

We see then that **preaching the Gospel** and **baptizing** are the two things which the Lord charged His disciples to do. Baptizing is put on the same level with preaching the Gospel, and second only to it. Moreover, it is connected directly with believing the Gospel as a condition of being "saved."* In view of these simple and

---

*For the meaning of the word "saved" in this passage, see p. 44.

plain words it would be difficult to overestimate the importance of baptism.

WHO ARE TO BE BAPTIZED?

We need not seek beyond the Lord's own words in order to obtain a sure answer to this question. The words "he that **believeth** and is **baptized** shall be saved," clearly indicate that believers of the Gospel were those who should be baptized. The language is clear and precise. Its meaning is readily apprehended by common people. Scholarship and profound studies into the types and shadows of the Old Testament cannot help us here, and such help is not needed. Only by doing violence to the language used by the Lord can room be made for the baptizing of any who have not heard and believed the Gospel.

The Gospel was to be preached to all. It was foreseen that some would believe, and that others would disbelieve, that is, would reject the message. The former were to be baptized, thereby securing the promised salvation. The words chosen by the Lord for conveying His last command, and which were recorded by the Holy Spirit so that they might stand as the age-long directions for His disciples, effectually exclude from baptism all except those who **hear** the Gospel of Christ and **believe** it. Not without setting aside the very words of the Lord by which baptism was appointed, can any be baptized except believers of the Gospel. Indeed we may confidently assert that, though others than believers may be immersed in water with the appropriate words, that act would not be baptism.

The commission of Christ to His disciples, as recorded in Matt. xxviii. 19, is no less explicit and clear. They were to go, and to make disciples of all nations. The method of making disciples was manifestly by preaching the Gospel of Christ crucified and risen from the dead. There was, and is, no other way. Those who became disciples through hearing and believing the Gospel were to be baptized, and also were to be taught to observe the things which Christ had commanded. No authority whatever has been given for baptizing others than those who had become disciples of Christ. The order is, first, making disciples; second, baptizing; third, teaching the Lord's commandments. Men have no more authority to change the order of the things appointed by the Lord than to change the things themselves. Departure from this command of the Lord is departure in respect to that which He has made of fundamental importance in carrying on His work in this age. Yet it is manifest that the departure has been great and well-nigh universal throughout Christendom. This is, no doubt, the cause of much of the evil that has befallen the Church.

THE BAPTISM OF JOHN

Baptism was not a novelty when the disciples of Jesus Christ began, at Pentecost, to baptize those who "gladly received the Word" that was preached to them, and that called them to repentance and faith in the risen Jesus. On the contrary, the significance of baptism, as having to do with **the sins of confessed sinners**, had been made thoroughly known in all Judea and the adjacent regions, through the ministry of John the Baptist. So profound was the impression made by the preaching and ministry of that prophet, than whom none greater had arisen among them that are born of women (Matt. xi. 11), that there "went out to him Jerusalem, and all Judea, and all the region round about Jordan, and were baptized of him in Jordan, confessing their sins" (Matt. iii. 5, 6); and, moreover, "all men mused in their hearts of John whether **he** were the Christ, or not" (Luke iii. 15).

The special ministry of John was to "**prepare the way of the Lord.**" This was the most important ministry ever committed to man. Put with this the fact that John was, by the Spirit Himself, designated "**the Baptizer,**" and we have at once a powerful Divine testimony to the importance of baptism.

The "way of the Lord" which John was to prepare was the way of **death, burial,** and **resurrection.** "Thus" was the Son of God "to fulfil all righteousness" (Matt. iii.

15). This way of righteousness was in view when the Spirit of Christ, through the Psalmist, said, "Burnt offering and sin offering hast Thou not required. Then said I, Lo, I come: in the Volume of the Book it is written of Me, I delight to **do Thy will**, O My God" (Ps. xl. 6-8; Heb. x. 5-7). This **will of God** which Christ delighted to do was the mighty work of redemption accomplished by His sufferings, death, and resurrection. And that is what His baptism symbolized.

The "Way of the Lord," for the accomplishment of His mighty plan with reference to man, necessitated the removal, by death, of the natural man, the "grass" humanity, as predicted by Isaiah in the prophecy foretelling the coming of John (Isa. xl. 6-8). "Flesh and blood cannot inherit the kingdom of God" (1 Cor. xv. 50). Hence, when the kingdom was about to be proclaimed, the Forerunner appeared on the scene; and his part was to prepare the way in symbol by putting confessed sinners into the waters of burial. Thus the ground was cleared for God to bring in His new humanity, born of water and the Spirit.

And not only did John proclaim baptism for confessed sinners, who thereby "justified God" in His condemnation of sin (Luke vii. 29), but he proclaimed also "the axe" of judgment laid at the root of the "trees." By the "trees" we understand John meant those who lifted themselves up in the pride of self-righteousness, refusing to be baptized as sinners. Those who do not voluntarily **come** down into the **water**, must be "**hewn** down and cast into the **fire**" (Matt. iii. 10).

But John had even a greater thing to do in the baptizing of the Lord Jesus, who came all the way from Galilee to Jordan expressly to be baptized of John (Matt. iii. 13). Thus He humbled Himself to take a place among the transgressors. John realized that Jesus should not be in that company, as is evidenced by the fact that he "forbade Him." And thereupon the Lord gave a most striking testimony to the significance and importance of baptism in those remarkable words, "Suffer (it to be so) now: for **thus** it becometh us to fulfil all righteousness." We learn from this saying that baptism is identified with that mighty work of God by which **all righteousness is fulfilled.** It would be well for the reader to pause here and ponder this great saying of the Lord Jesus.

Then followed the baptism of the Lord Jesus Christ, which was necessary before He entered upon the work the Father gave Him to do. His baptism definitely committed Him to the accomplishment of that work through the sufferings of the Cross (Luke xii. 50; John xix. 30).

The record states that "Jesus, when He was baptized, went up straightway out of the water"; and this emergence from the waters of burial, typifying His mighty resurrection, was signalized by a most wondrous event. "The heavens were opened unto Him, and He saw the Spirit of God descending like a dove, and lighting upon Him. And lo, a Voice from heaven saying, 'This is My Beloved Son, in whom I am well pleased.' "

Thus we find **connected with baptism** the **only** instance on record of the appearance on earth, in an articulate way, of the Three in whose "Name" (note the singular number "Name," not "Names") the Lord has commanded that believers in Him should be baptized (Matt. xxviii. 19).

Thus the ministry of John teaches us the deep significance and vast importance of baptism.

In this connection we would direct attention to Luke vii. 24-30. We find there the record of the Lord's testimony concerning John that he was truly the forerunner prophesied by Malachi (Mal. iii. 1), and that among those born of women there had not risen a greater prophet than he. Then comes the following statement:—

"And all the people that heard him, and the publicans, **justified God,** being baptized with the baptism of John. But the Pharisees and lawyers **rejected the counsel of God against themselves**, being not baptized of him."

This teaching is of the utmost importance. The sinners who submitted to be baptized **justified God** thereby. Whereas those who were not baptized rejected the counsel of God against themselves. This tells us clearly what is involved in the act of baptism, the capital point being that it has a **Godward aspect.** As the Apostle

Peter writes, it is "the demand of a good conscience **toward God**" (1 Pet. iii. 21). It justifies God in His dealings with the sinner. It declares that **God is just in decreeing the death of the man who has sinned.**

Thus the baptism of John symbolically cleared the scene of all human efforts to attain righteousness and salvation. It brought to the ground, and buried out of sight, all attempts at the betterment of the old nature. It declared the utter failure of all such efforts, even when the efforts were those of a selected people, aided by the holy law of God. It thus prepared the way for *God's* righteousness and *God's* salvation, also foretold by Isaiah in many passages (see Isa. li. 5-8, lii, 7-liii. 12, etc.), which the Servant of Jehovah was to accomplish by means of His atoning death and His resurrection.

In the baptism of John there is no mention of the emergence of any of those who were baptized except in the case of the Lord Jesus. Thus we get no hint of the resurrection in the inspired record of John's baptism except in the baptism of the Lord. Then the symbol of Resurrection comes clearly into view in the significant words, "And Jesus, when HE was baptized, **went up straightway out of the water.**"

Following this prophetic symbol of His resurrection occurred that wondrous event, by which God announced the presence on earth of a Man of a new order, a Man upon whom the Spirit of God could alight, and could **abide on Him** (John i. 32, 33), and whom the Voice of

God Himself declared to be the well-beloved Son. And this was at His baptism.

But the words, they "justified God," reach farther yet. God, in justifying the sinner, **must Himself be justified.** God's righteousness must be cared for. There must be no flaw upon it. If He forgives, He must do it according to strict justice, which permits no wrong-doing to go unpunished. Hence, in the passage which unfolds God's work of grace in justifying the believing sinner, through the redemption that is in Christ Jesus, we find that "the righteousness of God" is the prominent thing, being mentioned four times in the six verses (Rom. iii. 21-26). The Lord Jesus Himself said, in submitting Himself to be baptized of John, "**Thus** it becometh Us to fulfill **all righteousness.**" It was by His death that **all** righteousness was to be fulfilled. For it was "in His **blood**" (which signifies a life taken by violence) that God was "to declare His righteousness," not only "for the remission of sins that are **past,** through the forbearance of God," but also "to declare **at this time** His righteousness, that He might be **just,** and the justifier of him which believeth in Jesus." "THUS" did Christ justify God in forgiving sins committed in time past, as well as in the time that was yet to come. "**All** righteousness" was thus fulfilled.

And now the believing sinner, whom God has justified upon the righteous ground of the Redemption that is in Christ Jesus, is called upon to **justify God** in so doing.

For the believing sinner, by being baptized, is baptized into the **death of Christ** (Rom. vi. 3); and by that act he declares that **in no other way than by the death of Jesus Christ** could his sins be righteously pardoned. From this we may learn that baptism is necessarily an individual and a **voluntary** act. Let the reader judge for himself whether it be not a matter of the very first importance that he should be joined in the death of Christ, and be a partaker of the benefits thereof. That is what baptism signifies according to the clear teaching of Rom. vi. 3.

Consideration of these Scriptures makes it very plain why God has given to baptism a place of such peculiar importance in Christian doctrine and practice.

THE PRACTICE OF THE APOSTLES

The later New Testament Scriptures which mention baptism are, of course, in full accord with the Lord's own words spoken in appointing it. The practice of the disciples conformed to the command of their Lord. Were it not so, we should be constrained to disregard the practice and obey the command. We have, however, the threefold testimony of, **first,** the Lord's own directions; **second,** the practice of the Apostles directly guided by the Holy Spirit, as recorded in the Acts; and **third,** the doctrine concerning baptism given in the Epistles. These three several testimonies are in perfect agreement.

The very same day the Holy Spirit descended upon the disciples they proceeded to carry out the Lord's command, doing it in the energy of the Divine Spirit and under His control. Therefore, we may be absolutely certain that what is recorded of the acts of the Apostles on the day of Pentecost will afford us Divine instruction as to the details of baptism. Peter preached the Word, announcing the Resurrection of Jesus Christ. Those who **heard** were pricked in their heart, and asked, "What shall we do?" Then Peter said to them, "Repent, and be baptized every one of you in the Name of Jesus Christ for the remission of sins, and ye shall receive the Holy Ghost." Thereupon they that "**gladly received his Word** were baptized."

Here we have the preaching of the Gospel, and its effect in the **hearts** of those who heard it, causing them to turn to the Lord (that is, to repent). Having thus become disciples of Him who lately had been rejected by the whole nation, they were baptized in (literally **upon**) His Name. There was no delay about it. No study in the doctrine and typical significance of baptism was necessary. They were not put upon their probation. It was done "the same day" (Acts ii. 37-41).

Such was the invariable practice. The Gospel was preached, announcing the Resurrection of the Crucified One; and thereupon those who on hearing **believed,** were straightway baptized, and were thus "added" to the company of Christians. **Believing** is the only and the indispensable qualification for baptism.

Shortly thereafter Philip went down to Samaria "and preached Christ unto them" (Acts viii. 5). And "when they **believed** Philip preaching the things concerning the Kingdom of God, and the Name of Jesus Christ, they were baptized, both men and women" (ver. 12). They **heard** the Gospel, they **believed,** they were **baptized.** And to make the matter more clear, it is said, "both men and women." No infants or children are mentioned here or elsewhere.

In the next verse we read, "Then Simon himself **believed** also; and when he was baptized, he continued with Philip," etc. Some speak of Simon Magus as a "mere professor." If he were, it would afford no warrant for baptizing unbelievers. But it is distinctly said that Simon "believed" and was "baptized"; and the Lord's words were, "He that believeth and is baptized shall be saved." Hence we must regard Simon as a "saved" man. Simon's desire for the power to confer the Holy Spirit upon others, and his offer of money to obtain that power, do not prove he was an unconverted man. Many evil desires enter the hearts of converted persons, especially while young in the faith. Nor do Peter's words prove that Simon was an unconverted man. Rather the reverse; for Peter exhorted him to repent and pray to God; if perhaps the thought of his heart might be forgiven him. Such a remark could not appropriately be addressed to an unconverted man. What an unregenerate person needs is, not to pray to God that the evil thought of his heart be forgiven, but to repent and believe on the Lord Jesus Christ. The words "thou hast neither part nor lot in this matter" manifestly mean part and lot in the laying on of hands. The authority to give the Holy Ghost through the laying on of hands belonged to the Apostles only.

In the same chapter Philip joins the Ethiopian who, while journeying through the desert, was reading Isaiah liii. Thereupon Philip **preached** unto him Jesus. The Ethiopian manifestly believed the preaching, for he asked to be baptized, which request was granted. It was not until Philip had baptized the Ethiopian that the Spirit caught him away. This shows that, **until that command of the Lord had been carried out,** Philip's ministry was not completed. Here is a clear lesson for those who preach the Gospel in the present day. The unusual importance of this incident is indicated by the fact that the Holy Spirit dealt directly with Philip three times in the course of it. (1) He sent Philip to the very spot (ver. 26); (2) He directed him as to details what he should do (ver. 29); (3) He caught him away immediately after the baptism, showing Divine approval of the performance of that rite without an intervening period of probation (ver. 39). Manifestly it is an usurpation of authority for any one to interpose delay in the baptizing of one who confesses his faith in Christ.

In Acts ix., Saul of Tarsus, having been converted, arose and was baptized so soon as a disciple came to him (ver. 18). Although Saul had been fasting for three days he did not postpone being baptized until he had eaten (vers. 9, 19).

In Acts x. we read of the first formal proclamation of the Gospel to a company of Gentiles. The company was gathered at the house of Cornelius. To them Peter, having been expressly sent by the Holy Spirit, and after special preparation for his ministry, preached to them the good news of Christ risen from the dead, announcing forgiveness of sins through His Name to all who **believe** on Him. Thereupon the Holy Spirit fell upon "all them which heard the Word." This was a remarkable inversion of the usual order, according to which baptism with the Spirit followed baptism in water. But the reason appears. Peter would doubtless have hesitated to baptize Gentiles into the Divine Name. But the pouring out of the Holy Spirit upon them marked them clearly as fit subjects for water-baptism. So Peter said, "Can any man forbid **the water** (definite article in the original, meaning the baptismal water) that these should not be baptized, which have received **the Holy Ghost** as well as we? And he commanded them to be baptized in the Name of the Lord."

In this case also, as in the cases previously noticed, baptism was administered so soon as the preached

Word was believed. And again the Holy Spirit made it very manifest that the ministry of the preacher was not completed until he had baptised the believers.

We come now to the ministry of Paul. In Acts xvi. 14 we read that the Lord opened the **heart** of Lydia, that she attended unto the things spoken by Paul; and that when she was baptized and her household, she invited the apostles Paul and Silas to abide at her house. It is conjectured by some that Lydia's "household" included infants or other unconverted persons, and that such also were baptized. But there is not the slightest indication that either of these surmises is correct. She was a business woman carrying on a commercial enterprise in her own right—a strong proof that she was unmarried. Moreover, she was away from her home, which was in Thyatira. But we should not in any case rest upon a mere conjecture, however probable. Shall the unwarranted conjectures that there were unconverted persons in Lydia's household, and that they were baptized, be taken as a valid reason for departing from the directions given by the Lord?

There is, moreover, nothing to show that the word "house" or "household," as used in the Scriptures which speak of the baptism of households, necessarily includes infants, where there are any. The words of the angel to Cornelius indicate the sense in which this word is used. He bade Cornelius send for Peter, "who shall tell thee words, whereby thou and **thy house** shall be saved" (Acts xi. 14). We know that the words of salvation brought by Peter embraced the Gospel of Christ (which could not be preached to infants) and the command to be baptized. The Holy Spirit fell upon those who "heard the Word," and **they** were baptized. Thus the promise, "thou and thy house shall be saved," was fulfilled. This was strictly in accordance with the Lord's word recorded in Mark xvi. 16, "He that believeth and is baptized shall be saved."

The case of the Philippian jailer and his house is another instructive incident. To him the promise was given, "**Believe** on the Lord Jesus Christ, and thou shalt be **saved**, and **thy house**" (Acts xvi. 31). Then the Holy Spirit caused it to be recorded for our instruction how this promise was fulfilled; and we see that this again was in strict accordance with the word of the Lord Jesus, "He that **believeth** and is **baptized** shall be **saved.**". To this end first "they spake unto him the word of the Lord, and **to all that were in his house.**". This shows that **all** that were in his house were old enough to hear and understand the word of the Lord. Then, without so much as waiting for the morning, he "was baptized, he **and all his, straightway.**" After that he brought the Apostles into his house, and set food before them, "and rejoiced, **believing in God with all his house.**"

So the Word was preached to the jailer and all his

house, he was baptized and all his house, and he rejoiced, believing with all his house. Thus he and all his house were "saved." Dare we say that their obedience in respect to baptism had nothing to do with their salvation?

Again, in Acts xviii. 8 we read that, as the result of Paul's preaching in Corinth, "many of the Corinthians **hearing, believed,** and were **baptized.**"

Thus, in every case, the directions given by the Lord were faithfully carried out. Believing on the Lord Jesus was followed immediately by baptism. Indeed, **believing on** Him itself involves **obedience to His commands.** For **obedience** is the manner in which **faith** expresses itself. And where is obedience to begin if not at baptism? Will anything supply the lack of obedience to this fundamental and primary command? It may be objected that it is written that, "If thou shalt confess with thy mouth the Lord Jesus, and believe in thine heart that God raised Him from the dead, thou shalt be saved" (Rom. x. 9). But the omission of a reference to baptism in this Scripture cannot be taken to imply that baptism is unnecessary; for it must be remembered that Paul was writing to **baptized Christians,** not to unconverted persons. If they believed in their hearts in the Risen Christ, they would not have refused to be baptized in His Name.

In Acts xix. we read that Paul came to Ephesus and

found there certain disciples. He said to them, "Have ye received the Holy Ghost since ye believed?" And they said unto him, "We have not so much as heard whether there be any Holy Ghost." Paul immediately recognized that the fault lay **in the matter of baptism**; for he asked, "Unto what then were ye baptized?" And they said, "Unto John's baptism." This shows that one who has believed and **been baptized according to the command of Christ** should have **received the Holy Spirit.** To have believed, and to have become disciples, is not enough; for these were "disciples," and they had "believed," as appears by the words "since ye believed." To have believed and been **baptized, otherwise than as Christ commanded,** is not enough. Those Ephesian disciples had not been baptized into the Name of the Father and of the Son and of the Holy Ghost, or they would not have been ignorant of the existence of the Holy Ghost.

Thereupon Paul declared that John's baptism was preparatory to faith in Christ who was to come. "John truly baptized with a baptism of repentence, saying unto the people that they **should believe** on Him which **should come after him,** that is, on Christ Jesus." This agrees with John's own words, "I indeed baptize you with water **unto** repentance: but He that **cometh after me** is mightier than I, whose shoes I am not worthy to bear: He shall baptize you with the Holy Ghost, and with fire" (Matt. iii. 11). The Scriptures make it clear that John's entire ministry was **preparatory** to the Lord's coming. He was sent to "prepare the way of the Lord." Those who came to him confessing their sins were baptized, in preparation **for** ("unto") repentance and faith in the Coming One. The baptism commanded by Christ was **consequent upon** repentance and faith. **"Repent ye, and** be baptized every one of you, in the name of Jesus Christ for the remission of sins, and ye shall receive the Holy Ghost" (Acts ii. 38). There is manifestly a difference between John's baptism and Christ's. If it were not so, Paul would not have commanded those "disciples" to be re-baptized. But beyond all doubt there is a far greater difference between the baptism of infants and Christian baptism. For those baptized by John's baptism did confess their sins with a view to believing on One coming after. But infants cannot confess sins, or have anything in view.

So, finally, the incident teaches us that a baptism which **preceded faith** in Christ crucified and risen from the dead (John's baptism), even though it were a baptism which had been Divinely appointed for a season, will not avail as a substitute for baptism in the Name of the Father and of the Son and of the Holy Ghost, which must be **after** repentance and faith in the risen Saviour, as commanded by the Lord Jesus. Hence the baptism of infants or other unconverted persons will not avail to accomplish the purposes of Christian baptism, **or to secure its benefits to the baptized.** And who would be willing to incur a risk in a manner of such importance?

THE SIGNIFICANCE OF BAPTISM

BAPTISM AND THE RESURRECTION

We turn now to the Epistles, which teach us the spiritual significance of baptism.

The first, and the fullest of all, is Rom. vi. 3, 4. Baptism is there given prominence in answer to the question, "Shall we continue in sin?" The answer is given in the emphatic form of another question, which in effect is this: "How is it possible for us to continue in sin, seeing that **we who were baptized into Christ Jesus** were **baptized into His death?**" "**Baptized into Christ Jesus**," "**Baptized into His death!**" Do we grasp the tremendous import and deep solemnity of these words? What can possibly signify more to us, while yet in the mortal body—conversion alone excepted—than to be immersed* into the death of the Lord Jesus Christ? How is it possible, in the light of this Scripture, for any to regard baptism as of little importance? or for any to

---

*I do not stop to show that baptism is immersion. It would be too much like stopping to prove that baptism is baptism. Baptism is the act of temporarily putting under, or burying in, water. Hence it appropriately represents burial and resurrection.

entertain the thought that baptism could be for others than those who have been born from above, and hence have received life from Christ? This Scripture says, "So many of **us**," that is to say, saints, believers in Christ, "as were baptized." The terms of this Scripture exclude all who are not "of us."

To be immersed into all that the death of God's Son effected! Mighty fact. But the full significance of baptism has not yet been stated; for a greater fact has yet to be mentioned. "Therefore we are (were) buried with Him by baptism into death; that **like as Christ was raised up from the dead by the glory of the Father, even so we also should walk in newness of life.**"

We, believers who have been baptized, were **buried with Christ** by baptism into death (the place into which He went, but of which He **now has the key**), to the end that, **like as** He was raised up from among the dead by the glory of the Father, **even so** we also should walk this present scene in the newness of His resurrection life. The "we should walk" obviously designates the same persons as the "we are (were) buried." Since it is manifestly impossible that infants or other unconverted persons could walk in newness of life, this Scripture makes the baptism of such persons an impossibility. They may be put into water, or have water sprinkled upon them, but such ceremony would not be baptism.

The words "baptized into **His** death" pour a flood of light upon the meaning baptism. To be baptized into our own death would leave us for ever in the place of the dead, that is to say, in the place of eternal condemnation. But we have been baptized into the death of Another, Who died in our stead, even the death of that One Whom God has already **raised from the dead.** The Gospel that is preached to perishing sinners who are under the power of sin and death, announces Salvation through One Who died unto sin, and whom God has raised from the dead. They who, through the preaching of the Gospel, come to believe on the Risen One for their salvation, are forthwith baptized into His death, and are made sharers of His Resurrection. The rite thus corresponds perfectly with the facts; and, therefore, Christian baptism is the entrance, by the gateway of Christ's death, into the domain of **His** righteousness and life. The sins which were laid upon Him, and for which He suffered on the Cross, have all been dealt with judicially. Those sins were ours. The death **He** died was **our** due. He not only suffered for our sins, but He was "made sin for us," and died to **sin.** By baptism we were buried with Him into death, in order that, like as Christ was raised up from among the dead ones by the glory of the Father, **we also** should no longer continue in sin or in the state and place of **death,** but should walk in newness of **life.**

Baptism, then, is not a symbol merely of burial with Christ, but of **resurrection also** with Him. In fact, the being joined in the likeness of His resurrection ("**like**

as") is the principal thing.

The wondrous truth revealed in this Scripture is contained in the Lord's parable of the "corn of wheat" (John xii. 24). "Verily, verily, I say unto you, Except a corn of wheat of fall into the ground and die, it abideth alone: but if it die, it bringeth forth much fruit." He, of course, was that Corn of Wheat. So long as He lived in this world as a Man of flesh and blood (Heb. ii. 14), He lived alone. None shared, or could share, His life and His perfect human nature. There could be no "baptism into Christ" until He had become the antitype of the kernal of wheat that falls into the ground and dies. Having submitted to the deep humiliation of death and burial, He is able not only to rise from among the dead, but also to "bring forth" from the place of death "much fruit." He Himself is **the** Resurrection and **the** Life (John xi. 25).

Thus we arrive at the fact that Baptism represents the Resurrection, that grandest and mightiest work of God, the work in which He put forth "the **exceeding greatness** of His power," "according to the working of His mighty power which He wrought in Christ when He raised Him from the dead" (Eph. i. 19, 20). Within the sweep of this stupendous "working of His mighty power" are included the countless hosts of the redeemed, who are "quickened together with Christ," they being the marvellous fruitage of that Corn of Wheat that fell into the ground and died.

This is the work foretold by the prophet Habakkuk (Hab. i. 5), quoted by the Apostle Paul (Acts xiii. 41): "Behold, ye despisers, and wonder, and perish: for I **work a work** in your days, a work which ye shall in no wise believe, though a man declare it unto you."

In the light of this truth, how marvellous are the foreshadowings of the Resurrection, God's mightiest work, which are to be seen in the "baptisms" of the Old Testament! We see the earliest shadow of it, and a strong one too, in the coming forth of the earth out of its burial-place beneath the waters, on the **third day** (Gen. i. 9). We see it in the ark of Noah bearing its living freight through storm and flood, and depositing them in safety on Mount Ararat "on the seventeenth day of the month," **three days** later than the date of the Passover, which represents the death of Christ as the Lamb of God (Gen. viii. 4). We see it in the passage of the Israelites, on the **third day** after the Passover, through the Red Sea, where (according to 1 Cor. x. 2) the "fathers" of Israel were baptized. We see it in the crossing of Jordan, where "after **three days**" the Ark of the Covenant of the Lord went before the people "until all the people were passed clean over Jordan" (Josh. iii. 3, 4, 17). And we see it most clearly of all in the unique experience of Jonah, the man who was "three days and three nights" in the belly of the great sea monster, and was brought forth alive out of the waters, on the **third day,** to become a messenger of God to the Gentiles.

Thus the Hand of our God, in forming His Holy Word, has firmly knit together therein Baptism and the Resurrection,—that foundation fact of Christianity and of Salvation; and this was done, and the truth was woven into the texture of scripture, long before Christ was born.

If we would ask what the resurrection means to God, we have only to pay attention to the fact that by resurrection He received back again from the place of death the Son of His love; and by resurrection He receives every one of the "many sons" whom He is bringing unto glory, every one of the "many brethren" over whom the Son of God will preside as "the First-born." All these are "the children of the Resurrection" (Luke xx. 36).

In the face of these facts of Scripture can we fail to recognize the towering importance of the rite of baptism? Is not the neglect of the rite an indication of the indifference which now prevails in many quarters to the mighty truth for which it stands?

Taking the passage in Rom. vi. just as it reads, without attempting to construe it, or to say it means this or that, we find the clear statement that those saints who are baptized into Christ Jesus are baptized into His death, and become partakers of His resurrection. They are the "much fruit" which He brings forth.

It would require a volume to set forth the importance

of baptism as shown by the context of this doctrinal passage. For the present we must be content with pointing out that baptism stands here in immediate connection with the passing of the believer from under the dominion and bondage of sin into the service God. And this relates specially to the "**mortal body.**" It is the **body** that is put under water; and the saint who has thus passed in symbol through the waters of death is called upon to yield himself to God as one who is **alive from the dead**; and the members of his body as instruments of righteousness unto God (Rom. vi. 13). Thus the burial by baptism is but preliminary to resurrection.

In this connection it is appropriate to refer also to Col. ii. 12 and 1 Pet. iii. 21, since those Scriptures confirm the statement that baptism signifies the mighty fact of **resurrection with Christ,** after burial with Him. Col. ii. 12 reads (giving the correct tenses of the verbs), "having been buried with Christ in baptism, in which also **ye were raised with Him** through faith of the working of God, who raised Him from among the dead." Baptism, therefore, not only signifies burial with Christ (which throws light on the expression of Rom. vi. 3, "baptized into His death"), but it is also an expression of the baptized one's **faith** that God has raised Him from the dead. This is the belief which, according to Rom. x. 9, is necessary in order to be "saved."

In the Epistle to the Colossians important teaching is

based on the fact of the saints having been baptized, and thus in baptism having been "raised with Christ through faith"; for the Apostle says, "If ye then be risen (or were raised) with Christ, seek those things that are above, where Christ sitteth on the right hand of God. Set your affection on things above, not on things on the earth" (Col. iii. 1, 2). It is not seen how this Scripture could be applied to believers who have not been baptized **as such,** and were not thereby raised with Him **"through faith."** Apparently it is addressed to such, and to none others. There seems to be no warrant for applying it promiscuously to all believers. It does not appear that any are said to be risen with Christ who were not baptized. It is true that in Eph. ii. 5, 6 it is said that God has quickened together with Christ those who were dead in sins, and raised them up together. But the pronoun "we" is used, and it is known that Paul himself was baptized immediately after his conversion, and that he impressed upon the saints at Ephesus the imperative need of baptism, by commanding them to be baptized in the name of the Lord, after they had already received John's baptism. Undoubtedly, therefore, the passage in Ephesians refers to baptized saints. It would seem from the references to baptism, found in the Epistles, that it was taken for granted that the saints addressed had all been baptized. To think otherwise would be to assume that the Apostle Paul was careless and indifferent as to this command of the Lord. The incident at Ephesus

(Acts xix. 1-7) is sufficient in itself to show his great carefulness in this matter.

Moreover, in Eph. iv. 4, 5, baptism is named as one of the seven great things that constitute the "unity of the Spirit." It is a legitimate inference that a saint should no more contemplate being left out of participation in the "one baptism," than out of participation in the one body, the one hope, the one Spirit, the one Lord, the one faith, the one God and Father of all. Surely, as we observe the connection in which baptism is here placed, it must be evident that God's estimate of its importance differs materially from that of current teaching.

In 1 Pet. iii. 20, 21 it is stated that in the ark eight souls were "**saved** by water"; and then the Apostle says, "The like figure whereunto baptism doth also **now save us** (not the putting away of the filth of the flesh, but the answer [or the demand] of a good conscience toward God), by the **resurrection of Jesus Christ**."

We cite this Scripture here only to point out the connection that baptism has with the resurrection of Jesus Christ. We shall have occasion to refer to it again for another purpose.

In 1 Cor. xv. 29 is a passage difficult of interpretation. There is, however, no difficulty in perceiving that it connects baptism very closely with the resurrection, which is the subject of the entire chapter. The verse reads: "Else what shall they do which are baptized for the dead, **if the dead rise not?** Why are they then baptized for the dead?" The suggestion is that the resurrection is what gives baptism its significance, and that apart from resurrection it would be meaningless.

Turning to Gal. iii. 26, 27 we read: "For ye are all the children of God by faith in Christ Jesus. **For** as many **of you** as have been baptized into Christ have **put on Christ.**"

Here again the thought connected with baptism is not merely that of death (which cuts one off from his old relationships), but that of a **new life and condition of being,** having new relationships. Indeed, death is not mentioned in this passage at all; the only consequence of baptism here stated being the **putting on of Christ.** This is truly a stupendous thing, insomuch that a determined effort of the mind is required in order to apprehend it even in a small measure. Is it not truly a great thing to "put on Christ"? How important then is **that act whereby Christ is put on!** Let the reader carefully ponder this. For even if he is a baptized believer, does he not owe a duty to the many Christians who, through neglect of this important command of the Lord, are now suffering great loss, and are in danger of suffering loss hereafter?

Let us carefully notice also the exactitude of Scripture. We have here, as in Rom. vi. 3, the expression "baptized into Christ." And again the Apostle is careful to say "as many **of you,**" just as in Rom. vi. 3 he said "as many **of us,**" thus limiting the described result of baptism to those of the **saints** who had been **baptized.** Indeed, it is obvious that none others could by any possibility "put on Christ." But, more than this, the truth that only believers can be baptized, is doubly guarded by ver. 26: "For ye are (ye exist as, or have come to be) the **sons of God** by faith in Christ Jesus." And ver. 27 connects with this by the word "for." It is thus absolutely certain that those who had **come to be** (the word "**are,**" in the original, has this force) **sons of God,** having been born from above, were the ones who, by baptism into Christ, had put on Christ. And furthermore, they had come to be "sons of God" by **faith** in Christ Jesus. They were **believers,** then. And I doubt not the passage (and others also which we have noticed) carried with it the implication that their "faith" in the risen Christ **had been manifested by obeying Him in the matter of baptism.**

Faith and obedience are closely akin. We have in the Scriptures the two expressions "believe the Gospel" and "obey the Gospel." Practically they mean the same thing; for they who truly believe the Gospel obey it. The closing passage of Romans resembles that of Matthew. The Apostle speaks of his Gospel and the preaching of Jesus Christ, made known to **all nations** for the **obedience of faith** (Rom. xvi. 25, 26). Also in the introductory part of the Epistle he speaks of the Gospel of God concerning His Son, Jesus Christ our Lord, by whom he had received apostleship for the **obedience of faith,** among **all nations,** on behalf of His Name (Rom. i.

1-4). This was the carrying out of the Lord's directions to make disciples out of **all nations,** baptizing them into the Divine Name, and teaching them obedience to all His commandments. Surely, obedience to the Gospel should begin where it began at Pentecost and in all Apostolic practice, namely, by burial with Christ in baptism.

Obedience to the Lord Jesus in the matter of baptism should be counted a great privilege. Yet the natural heart shrinks from it, and to many, if not to all, it is something of an ordeal. But let us call to mind **His** baptism of sufferings and death to which He referred when He said, "I have a baptism to be baptized with; and how I am straitened till it be accomplished!" (Luke xii. 50). From that baptism He did not shrink, but, "when the time was come that He should be received up, He stedfastly set His face to go to Jerusalem" (Luke ix. 51), fulfilling the word of Isaiah, "therefore have I set my face like a flint" (Isa. l. 7). Shall they who have received pardon and life through His baptism of suffering and death refuse obedience to His commandment, and hold back from being baptized into His death? Shall not the love of Christ constrain us?

DOCTRINES ASSOCIATED WITH BAPTISM

In the foregoing comments we have noticed

incidentally some of the important Christian doctrines which are directly associated in the New Testament Scriptures with baptism. Especially have we pointed out the connection between baptism and the Resurrection. But we believe it will well repay us to observe more closely these associated doctrines, since we may thereby gain the knowledge of important truth.

BAPTISM AND THE NAME OF THE LORD

Attention should be given to the connection between baptism and the Name of the Lord. The Lord's directions are that those who are made disciples should be baptized **to, unto,** or **into** the Name of the Father, and of the Son, and of the Holy Ghost. He does not say the "names," as of three, but the **Name,** as of One.

The words of Paul in 1 Cor. x. 1, 2 will help us to understand this. He there says that the "fathers" of the Israelites who crossed the Red Sea were "all baptized **unto** Moses in the cloud and in the sea." The preposition rendered "unto" (*eis*) is the same as in Matt. xxviii. 19. We may therefore infer that just as the Israelite fathers were, by baptism in the cloud and in the Red Sea, cut off from the authority of Pharaoh, and committed to the authority and care of Moses, so the believing sinner is, by his baptism, cut off from the world (which Egypt represents typically) and is committed to the authority and care of God.

In Peter's exhortation at Pentecost he said, "Repent, and be baptized every one of you in the Name of Jesus Christ for the remission of sins." Here there is a different preposition (*epi*), signifying "upon" the Name of Jesus Christ . This conveys the thought of "upon the authority" of His Name. The Apostles were acting wholly "in the Name of Jesus Christ," that is to say, they referred to Him as the source of all the authority by which they acted. (See Acts iii. 6, 16, iv. 7, 10, 17, 18, etc.) Peter had announced in his discourse the great fact that "God hath made that same **Jesus** whom ye crucified, both **Lord** and **Christ**" (ii. 36). Therefore, whatever was commanded upon the authority of His Name was to be obeyed.

Peter's command to the Jews to be baptized **upon** the Name of Jesus Christ is not in conflict with, nor to be taken as setting aside, the Lord's directions to baptize believers **into,** or **unto,** the Name of the Father, and of the Son, and of the Holy Ghost. It was the setting up of Jesus Christ as the source of the authority in virtue of which the Jews were called upon to repent and be baptized. All Christian baptism is unto the Name of the Father, and of the Son, and of the Holy Ghost. The believer in Jesus Christ is brought **into** all the privilege and blessing that pertains to the fulness of the Deity as represented by that Name. The Name of the Father, and of the Son, and of the Holy Ghost, expresses what

Christianity is, in a way that is expressed by no other form of words.

We should compare the words of Peter in Acts ii. 38, which were recorded by the same inspired writer—"And that **repentance** and the **remission of sins** should be preached **in His Name,** among all nations, beginning at Jerusalem" (Luke xxiv. 47). Note the exact correspondence with the expressions used by Peter, "repentance," "remission of sins," "in His Name." And the correspondence is the more complete because in Luke xxiv. as in Acts ii. the words are "**upon** His Name." Thus, we see in Acts ii. the "beginning at Jerusalem" of the fulfilment of the Lord's commands which are to be carried out, from that starting-point, among "all nations."

We deem it very important to note that the record in Acts ii. supplies the fact, not mentioned in Luke's Gospel as in Matthew and Mark, that baptism had a place in the Lord's parting commands for the age. They were to preach repentance and baptism for (*eis*, unto) the remission of sins, upon the authority of the Name of Jesus Christ.

In Acts viii. 12 we read that "when they believed Philip preaching the things concerning the kingdom of God, and the **Name of Jesus Christ,** they were baptized, both men and women." Here again the Name of the Lord Jesus is closely associated with baptism.

In the case of Saul of Tarsus (Acts xxii. 16), Ananias

bade him "arise and be baptized, and wash away thy sins, calling **upon the Name of the Lord.**" Thus we see that baptism is in effect a "calling upon the Name of the Lord." Are we not therefore warranted in assuming that there is an indirect reference to baptism in Rom. x. 13, "For whosoever shall call upon the Name of the Lord shall be saved"?

In Acts x. 43, Peter announced to the company assembled in the house of Cornelius that "**through His Name** whosoever believeth in Him shall receive **remission of sins.**" At that moment his utterance was cut off by the Holy Spirit coming in Person and making it plain to Peter that baptism was to be immediately given to those who heard the word of **remission of sins** through **His Name.** Accordingly Peter "commanded them to be baptized **in the Name of the Lord**" (ver. 48). The word here is not "upon the Name of **Jesus Christ,**" nor is it "unto the Name"; but "in (*en*) the Name of the Lord."

In the case of the disciples at Ephesus who had been already baptized, the question was, "**Unto** (*eis*) what then were ye baptized?" (Acts xix. 3). Inasmuch as they had not received the Holy Spirit it was evident to Paul that they had not been baptized **unto** the Name of the Father, and of the Son, and of the Holy Ghost. Thereupon, having heard what Paul said about John's baptism, "they were baptized in (unto) **the Name of the Lord Jesus.**" And then Paul laid his hands on them and they received the Holy Ghost.

It seems proper to connect this with what Paul subsequently wrote to those same Ephesian saints. He had asked them, "Have ye received the Holy Ghost since ye believed?" And they had said, "We have not so much as heard whether there be any Holy Ghost." Consequently, the event was a momentous one to them. In his letter, Paul uses the same expression as used in his question when he met them, saying, "In whom (Christ) ye also trusted after that ye heard the word of truth, the gospel of your salvation, in whom also **after that ye believed** ye were **sealed with that Holy Spirit of Promise**" (Eph. i. 13). This is a manifest reference to the time "when they heard" and "were baptized unto the Name of the Lord Jesus," and "the Holy Ghost came upon them."

From this we learn, as from other Scriptures, that the believing of these disciples in the Lord Jesus included being baptized in His Name.

So we have these three expressions in connection with baptism: "baptized **upon** the Name of Jesus Christ" (Acts ii. 38); "baptized **in** the name of the Lord" (x. 48); and "baptized **unto** the Name of the Lord Jesus" (xix. 5).

This association of Baptism with the Name of the Lord should deeply impress our hearts with the importance of that rite.

BAPTISM AND SALVATION

The Lord's own command distinctly makes baptism one of the things upon which salvation in some sense depends. "He that believeth and is baptized shall be saved" (Mark xvi. 16). In view of these words we dare not say that baptism is not essential to salvation. But it is very important to understand the meaning of the word "saved" in this Scripture. There is danger of misunderstanding at this point because of the fact that the word "salvation" has come to mean, in current thought and speech, the pardon and reconciliation of the sinner, and the bestowal upon him of the gift of eternal life. That is generally what is meant when it is said that a person has been "saved." But the word "salvation" is not so used in Scripture; for the forgiveness and acceptance of the sinner does not depend upon his obedience, or upon any words of his own, but solely and wholly upon the work of Christ for him. The finished work of Christ, and that alone, is sufficient for the justification of every believing sinner, and for his eternal deliverance from all the consequences of sin, and of his own sins. As to that, there is no doubt whatever. Therefore, in seeking to ascertain what baptism has to do with salvation, it must be remembered that the words "saved" and "salvation" have not always the same meaning in Scripture. Sometimes salvation is used as synonymous with justification, which is, by the grace of God, given to all that believe (Acts x. 43; xiii. 38, 39; Rom. iii. 21-26, etc.). Sometimes it means saved from the wrath to come, from the judgment of the wicked, and from the lake of fire (1 Thess. i. 10). Sometimes it means being saved day by day from enemies, trials, and temptations (Isa. lxiii. 9). Sometimes it means being saved alive to enter the Kingdom of Christ (Matt. xxiv. 13, "He that shall endure to the end, the same shall be **saved**"). When "salvation" is used in any of the above senses it does not depend upon baptism. But the word "saved" sometimes refers to a present position of privilege, as being brought into the death and resurrection of Christ, or as the putting on of Christ. Furthermore, it refers also to something specially to be revealed at the Coming of the Lord Jesus, and which is dependent upon faithfulness and obedience. Thus Peter speaks of being "kept by the power of God **through faith** unto the **salvation** ready to be revealed in the last time"; and again he says, "receiving the **end** of your **faith,** the **salvation** of your souls." For this salvation he bids us gird up the loins of our mind, to be sober, and "hope **to the end** for the grace that is to be brought to us at the revelation of Jesus Christ" (1 Pet. i. 5, 9, 13). The Lord Himself spoke of a salvation that is dependent upon individual obedience and faithfulness. And baptism is certainly conspicuous among the matters in regard to which He should be obeyed. Those Scriptures give a hint as to the meaning of the statement "he that believeth and is baptized shall be saved." And it will be observed that all such Scriptures point to the coming Kingdom of Christ as the time when both obedience and disobedience on the part of God's people shall receive "a just recompense of reward" (Heb. ii. 2).

Salvation is first mentioned in Scripture at the crossing of the Red Sea. (The word itself occurs only once previously, Gen. xlix. 18, where Jacob says he had "waited" for it.) In Ex. xiv. 13 we read, "And Moses said unto the people, Fear ye not, stand still and see the **salvation of the Lord.**" And at ver. 30, after describing the passage through the waters, it is written, "Thus the Lord **saved** Israel that day out of the hand of the Egyptians." The waters which overwhelmed the Egyptians became the pathway for the Israelites into newness of life, a life with Christ in the wilderness. It is remarkable and instructive that the first occurrence of **salvation** in Scripture is in connection with the crossing of the Red Sea, at which time, as we learn by 1 Cor. x. 1, 2, the fathers of Israel were baptized unto Moses. This testifies strongly to the close connection between Baptism and Salvation.

Salvation, in its broadest and fullest sense, signifies the complete purpose of God for those whom He calls and justifies, and includes bringing them into their promised inheritance. In that broad sense salvation is not yet ours. It lies in the future, and becomes ours at the Resurrection. Hence the word "resurrection" carries with it the thought of full salvation; and baptism is the symbol of this.

But meanwhile we have the Holy Spirit, who is the "earnest" or "first-fruits" of our expected inheritance (Rom. viii. 23, 24; 2 Cor. v. 5; Eph. i. 13, 14). Hence the possession of the Spirit, who is life (Rom. viii. 10), and of the forgiveness of sins, are the main characteristics of salvation in its present stage; and it is of importance to note that baptism is very closely connected both with the receiving of the Spirit and with the forgiveness of sins. We shall refer at this point to some Scriptures which speak of baptism and the Holy Spirit, leaving the subject of remission of sins for another chapter.

BAPTISM AND THE HOLY SPIRIT

The possession of the Holy Spirit is a present phase of salvation which is, in the Scriptures, very closely related to baptism.

When the Lord Jesus enacted in symbol His own death and resurrection, by commanding and suffering John to put Him under the waters of Jordan; and when He came up straightway out of those waters of death and judgment, **then** the **Spirit of God** descended upon Him, and, lo, a voice from heaven saying, "This is My beloved Son, in whom I am **well pleased.**"

Here we have the example of the Obedient One; and
we have also the Father's expressed pleasure in that
which represented His obedience "unto death." This is
the representation, symbolically, of the truth that is
expressed in the title "First-born from the dead" (Col. i.
18; Rev. i. 5). The words of the second Psalm, here
voiced by the Father from heaven, apply to Christ as the
Risen One (Acts xiii. 33), the "first-fruits" to the Father
"from the dead." Since Christ is "the First-fruits," His
resurrection is the guaranty of the resurrection of all the
"many sons" whom God is bringing into glory. All
become the sons of God by **resurrection.** They are "the
children of God, **being the children of the resurrection**"
(Luke xx. 36). Moreover, we learn from these Scriptures
that resurrection is a **birth from the dead,** or **out of
death.** Baptism is the symbol of this birth from the place
of death.

Furthermore, this explanation is in harmony with the
teaching of Romans, Galatians, Colossians, and 1
Peter, which we have examined. So many of us (saints)
as have been baptized, were baptized into **His** (Christ's)
death, that is to say, the death figured at Jordan, where
He was numbered with those who confessed their sins,
and was treated like them (for thus He was "to fulfil all
righteousness"); and where He also **went up straightway
out of the water,** when the Spirit of God came upon Him,
and He was announced from heaven as Son of God. Into
that death and resurrection those who believe on Him,

having been already born from above, are baptized.

The association of baptism and the Spirit is seen again in Acts ii. 38: "Repent, and be **baptized** every one of you, and ye shall receive **the Holy Ghost.** For the promise is unto you, and to your children, and to all that are afar off, even as many as the Lord our God shall call."

Moreover, we read in the same Scripture, "And with many other words did he testify and exhort, saying, **Save yourselves** from this untoward generation. Then they that gladly received his word were baptized." Baptism was their response to the exhortation "Save yourselves." This Scripture seems clearly to make the promise of the Spirit to depend upon obedience in the matter of baptism. It also speaks of a sense in which those addressed were to save themselves. Obviously the salvation here referred to was limited in its nature. It was "from this untoward generation."

In the case of the Samaritans who believed and were baptized by Philip, the Holy Spirit did not fall upon them as soon as they were baptized (Acts viii. 16). But "when the Apostles who were at Jerusalem heard that Samaria had received the Word of God, they sent unto them Peter and John, who, when they were come down, prayed for them that they might receive the Holy Ghost. Then laid they their hands on them, and they received the Holy Ghost."

We cannot, perhaps, say with certainty why the Holy

Spirit, in His sovereign will, did not come upon the Samaritan believers immediately they were baptized. But, if we recall that those who were baptized at Pentecost were "added" to the Apostolic company, and that subsequently the Lord "added" to the Church such as were being saved (Acts ii. 41, 47), a reason may be perceived. There was need to impress upon all believers the great fact of the "one body," whereof the Apostles were the chief ministers. Hence when the despised Samaritans were converted, the Spirit appointed that the leading Apostles should go to Samaria, and by laying on of their hands, which signifies **identification** with the person on whom the hands are laid, make it manifest that the converted and baptized Samaritans were **added** to, and **identified** with, the Church which Christ was in process of building. There was to be "one body," into which every believer, regardless of his nationality, was to be baptized by the "One Spirit" (1 Cor. xii. 13; Eph. ii. 16, 18; Gal. iii. 28). This truth was taught by the incident at Samaria, and by that at Ephesus, referred to below. The coming of the Holy Spirit, simultaneously with this act whereby the Samaritan converts were expressly identified with the Church at Jerusalem, thus doing the exceedingly important and momentous thing of establishing a link between Jerusalem and Samaria, put the Divine Seal upon the act. There was need, in the case of the first Gentile converts, for some special action, under the immediate direction of the Holy Spirit, which should clearly show that those converts were fully admitted into the company of Christians along with Jewish converts; for at that time, as is recorded in John iv. 10, "the Jews had no dealings with the Samaritans"; and as to the Gentiles, they were "far off," being "aliens from the commonwealth of Israel, and strangers from the covenants of promise" (Eph. ii. 12).

So also at Ephesus, after the disciples there had been baptized, Paul laid his hands on them, thus formally identifying them with the Apostolic company; and thereupon the Holy Spirit came upon them, thus giving the Divine sanction to his action (Acts xix. 6). But in each of the foregoing cases baptism preceded the coming of the Holy Spirit, just as in the case of the Lord's own baptism. As already noted, there is an evident reference to this baptism of the Ephesian believers in Paul's letter to the Ephesians, where he reminds them that, after that they heard the word of truth, the gospel of salvation, they were sealed with the Holy Spirit of promise. By laying his hands upon them, thus formally identifying them with the Jewish believers, he symbolically testified the truth which is specially emphasized in Ephesians, namely, that the Gentiles who believe are no longer "far off," no longer aliens from the commonwealth of Israel and strangers from the covenants of promise, but of the same body, fellow-citizens with the saints and of the household of God (Eph. ii. 12, 19, 20).

It will be observed that, in the two recorded cases (Samaria and Ephesus) in which the hands of Apostles were laid upon the baptized believers before they received the Holy Ghost, there were exceptional circumstances; and surely we are warranted in assuming that the exceptional action was due to those exceptional circumstances. In all cases, however, without exception, there was a connection between Baptism and the receiving of the Holy Ghost.

In the case of the Gentile company at the house of Cornelius the record presents a very striking antithesis between "the water" and "the Spirit." When they had mainifestly received the Spirit, Peter put the question, "Can any man forbid **the** water that these should not be baptized who have received **the Holy Spirit** as well as we?" (Acts x. 47). In this case the coming of the Holy Spirit upon the believers preceded their baptism in water. But, so far was that from indicating that water-baptism was unnecessary that it was perceived by the Apostle Peter to be a reason why they should be forthwith baptized.

In Gal. iii. 2, Paul asks, "Received ye the Spirit by the works of the law or by the hearing of faith?" and he explains farther on (vers. 13, 14) that Christ was made a curse for us, in order that the blessing of Abraham might come on the Gentiles through Jesus Christ, "that we might receive **the promise of the Spirit** by **faith.**" Here is the same thing that Peter spoke of on the day of Pentecost, *i.e.* "the promise of the Spirit," which is received by "the hearing of **faith**." The fair inference seems to be that "the hearing of faith" embraced the hearing and obeying of the command regarding baptism, for in the case in Acts ii. it is recorded that "they that gladly **received his word** were baptized." This is confirmed by ver. 27 of Gal. ii.: "For as many of you as have **been baptized** into Christ have put on Christ."

Therefore, while there remains very much yet to be learned from these Scriptures, we can surely see that salvation, in some special sense, depends upon our rendering obedience in the matter of baptism. This salvation, in the time present, has something to do with receiving the Spirit for gift, and service, and for power to walk in newness of life; and in the age to come it has to do with the Kingdom. This much, it would seem, we may safely affirm. And we may well ask, Should it not be the normal experience of the believer, after baptism in water, to receive the Holy Spirit, with power and enduement in some measure for the purposes stated above?

Finally, as showing the connection between baptism and salvation, we refer again to 1 Pet. iii. 20, 21. In ver. 18 the death and resurrection of Christ are mentioned, and a special purpose of His sufferings is here set forth, namely, "that He might bring us to God." Manifestly, God could be reached only through death and resurrection, which is what baptism represents. It is also stated that He was "put to death in the flesh, but quickened by **the Spirit.**" Then, in the same sentence occurs the well-known reference to imprisoned spirits who were **disobedient** in the time when the long-suffering of God waited in the days of Noah, while the ark was in course of preparation, wherein few, that is, eight souls, were **saved by water,** the like figure whereunto even baptism doth also now save us (not a putting away of the filth of the flesh, but a demand of a good conscience toward God; **by the resurrection of Jesus Christ.** All this (vers. 18 to 21) is in **one sentence,** whereof the leading thought is that, like as the ark, enduring the flood and the storm of waters poured out from above, carried Noah and his family to a place of safety; so, Christ, who endured the water-floods and storm of wrath that was due to our sins, brings us to God. Noah, however, was saved by the **obedience of faith,** for it is written that "by **faith** Noah, being warned of God, prepared an ark to the **saving** of his house" (Heb. xi. 7). This again calls our attention to the important fact that **faith expresses itself in obedience.** What would Noah's belief in the warnings of God have availed, if he had not **obeyed** by building the ark in the face of all the opposition of the world of his day? And of what avail is it to those who believe in God now and call Christ "Lord," if they do not the things which He says? And why is this solemn lesson about Noah, with its reference to the spirits of those who **disobeyed** in his day, given to us in direct connection with baptism, which is a matter involving obedience? Is it supposed that disobedience is any less serious in those to whom abundance of grace and of the revelations of God have been given, than in the comparatively unenlightened antediluvians? Let this lesson be deeply pondered; for we shall all stand, and very shortly, before the judgment-seat of Christ, to receive of the things done in our bodies, each "according to that he hath done, whether it be good or bad" (2 Cor. v. 10).

Noah was "saved by water." The water carried the ark and its passengers to the top of a high mountain. We are saved "by the resurrection of Jesus Christ," which lifts us above the waters of death and judgment into the place of safety. This parallel is evident. But, beside this, Noah's faith and obedience were necessary to his salvation. If the building of the ark was a thing which Noah had to do in manifesting his faith and obedience, must we not conclude that baptism is something that we must do to manifest our faith and obedience? If Noah could not have dispensed with the ark, can Christians dispense with baptism?

BAPTISM AND SINS

The connection between baptism and sins is akin to

that between baptism and salvation. Nevertheless, it may be profitably considered under a separate heading.

The passage last cited (1 Pet. iii. 21) tells us more about baptism than was pointed out in the last chapter, namely, that it is not a putting away of the filth of the flesh, but the demand of a good conscience toward God. It is not a mere washing off of uncleanness from the surface of the body. It has to do with the **conscience.** This, we believe, explains the words of Ananias to Saul: "Arise, and be baptized, and wash away thy sins" (Acts xxii. 16). The sins which God has pardoned on the ground of Christ's atoning work should be **washed away.** The conscience that is "good" toward God demands this. No conscience that is enlightened by the Word of God would be satisfied without thus washing away the forgiven sins in the waters of judgment, into which Christ bore them in His own body. By this act the pardoned sinner identifies himself with Christ's death and resurrection, thus putting on Christ. We should have, not only our "hearts sprinkled from an evil conscience," but also "our bodies washed with pure water" (Heb. x. 22). This, as it seems to us, is "the washing of regeneration" (Tit. iii. 5), that is to say, the washing or cleansing which is symbolized by baptism. This "washing of regeneration" is here again coupled with the "renewing of the Holy Ghost." Newborn infants should be immediately washed (Ezek. xvi. 4). So those who are newly born from above receive a spiritual washing. Baptism is the symbol of this; and, from what the Scriptures plainly teach, it is clear that the symbol of this washing of regeneration may not be neglected without incurring serious loss, and probably severe discipline. It is thus with regard to the appointed symbols of the Lord's death. As was written to the Corinthian saints, "For this cause (not discerning the Lord's body) many are weak and sickly among you, and many sleep" (1 Cor. xi. 30).

We have lately seen, in a paper on baptism, the statement that Saul of Tarsus was commanded to wash away his sins "before men," as they were already "gone from before God." But we see no authority in Scripture for this statement. The words "before men" are an interpolation. Saul was not told to wash away his sins "before men." There is no evidence that any one was present except Ananias. On the other hand, Peter tells plainly that baptism is the demand of a good conscience **toward God.** This may, indeed, mean the demand which God makes of a good conscience toward Himself. But whether it is God who makes the demand or the conscience that makes it, the result is the same. For a good conscience will be in agreement with God, and will demand what He demands. The point is, that the aspect of baptism is primarily "towards God." Whatever force it may have as a testimony or confession of faith before men is incidental. And such a thought as washing away one's sins "before men" seems to be wholly unscriptural.

We gather from the Scriptures that the expression of Ananias to Saul, "wash away thy sins," signifies something quite distinct from what is meant (for example) by the words, "Unto Him that loved us and washed (or loosed) us from our sins in (or by) His own blood" (Rev. i. 5). The pardoning, remitting, removing, and putting away of our sins is, of course, the act of **God alone;** and its effective agent is the **blood of Christ.** As it is written, "Being now justified by His blood" (Rom. v. 9). "In whom we have redemption through His blood, the forgiveness (lit. remission) of sins according to the riches of His grace" (Eph. i. 7). Baptism, on the other hand, is the act of man, though in obedience to the command of God. Hence the washing away of Paul's sins, which he was commanded to do by baptism, was something distinct from the remission or forgiveness of sins. He had remission of sins from the moment of his conversion. But it is easy to see that there may remain to the believing sinner some stain or other consequence of sins that have been pardoned. If the proper reading of Rev. i. 5 is "loosed (or freed) from our sins," as some of the critical texts (Lachmann, Tischendorf, Tregelles, Alford, and others) have it, then obviously the sins from which one has been **loosed** could be **washed away.** On the other hand, until the sins have been loosed or pardoned by God they could not be washed away. Hence a form of baptism to one not justified by faith through the blood of Christ would be a vain ceremony.

Seemingly, then, baptism puts the pardoned sinner in a different light before God from that in which he stood before his baptism, the difference being of such a sort that it answers to the thought of washing away the sins that God has pardoned. Hence, to refuse to be baptized would indicate an indifference to the sins which God has so freely forgiven, and to the **great price** which the Son of God paid to secure His forgiveness.

One of the evil spiritual conditions of our day is the light estimation of the heinousness of sin. This is well-nigh universal. Vast numbers of nominal Christians make so little of sin that the necessity for the sufferings of Christ, in expiation thereof, is wholly set aside; and by some the doctrine of the atonement is even derided. The minds of others, even of those who hold the doctrine of the atonement, are much affected by this view; and one of the consequences is that they do not realize the importance, in God's sight, of going through the waters of baptism, thereby expressing, by the divinely appointed rite, that their sins deserved what their Saviour suffered in their stead, and what those waters symbolize, and thereby expressing also their faith in the operation of God who raised Him from the dead (Col. ii. 12).

Inasmuch as the Scriptures teach that baptism is closely connected with the sins of men, and also with the sufferings which Christ endured in consequence thereof, it is clearly a matter of exceedingly great importance. It follows of necessity that, for a pardoned sinner to refuse to pass through in symbol, what the Saviour passed through in reality, is a very serious offence against the authority of the Lord Jesus Christ, and against the holiness and righteousness of God, which demanded the sufferings and death of Christ as the price of the sinner's pardon and acceptance. And if the offence be serious, its consequences must be proportionately serious.

Consideration of these clear teachings of Scripture may help us to apprehend the thought expressed by the words "be baptized and wash away thy sins."

We write these lines in much concern for those pardoned sinners who have neglected baptism; for we greatly desire that they should give heed to this matter before it is too late, and be saved from the consequences of so grave an act of disobedience.

It is true, indeed, that believers in Christ are eternally delivered from the penalty of sin. They will never come into the judgment of the wicked dead, and are saved from eternal wrath and the lake of fire. But it yet remains to be seen what means the Lord will take with saints who refused to obey His command regarding baptism. That must await His judgment-seat, where "we shall **all** stand" (2 Cor. v. 10), and where "**every one** of us shall give an account of himself to God" (Rom. xiv. 10).

In Rom. vi. 2-10 we again see a direct connection

between baptism and sin. The question, "Shall we continue in sin?" is answered by the statement that we died to sin in that we were baptized into the death of Christ, who died unto sin once for all.

In Gal. iii. 22 it is declared that the law hath concluded all under sin, that the promise (of the Spirit? see ver. 14) might be given to them that believe. And this is followed by the statement that "as many of you as have been baptized into Christ have put on Christ" (ver. 27).

In Col. ii. 12, 13 we read, "Buried with Him in baptism, wherein also ye are risen with Him through the faith of the operation of God, who hath raised Him from the dead. And you, being dead **in your sins and the uncircumcision of your flesh,** hath He quickened together with Him, **having forgiven you all trespasses.**"

We attempt no exposition of these Scriptures. It is not necessary for our purpose. To accomplish that it is only needful to observe that not in one Scripture only, but in many, the forgiveness of sins and the washing away of sins are closely linked with baptism. This should move unbaptized believers to arise and make haste to obey the Lord's command. And it should admonish baptized believers not to be guilty of keeping silence in regard to this important matter.

It will, we think, be evident from what has been already said that we are not attributing saving virtue to a mere rite. In these pages we have sought not to give **our** opinion of the importance of baptism, but to allow the

Scriptures to **tell us** what is its importance in **God's** estimation. Indeed, we have finished this study with a far different estimate of the importance of baptism from that we had in entering upon it; for we were at that time much under the influence of current ideas. Therefore we would urge the reader to put aside the opinions and views of men on this subject, and diligently search the Scriptures for himself.

We attribute no virtue at all to the rite. The virtue lies wholly in **obedience.** Let us not forget that it was a single act of disobedience, in regard to what was seemingly a matter of little consequence, that caused the ruin of the human race, and filled the world with wickedness and misery (Rom. v. 19). It must needs be, therefore, that the disregard of a command which the Lord has made so prominent, and has connected so closely with His work of Redemption, will result in consequences of the utmost gravity to those who disobey.

INSTRUCTIONS FOR BAPTISM

Baptism is, as we have seen, a thing commanded by the Lord for "all nations," and for "all the days" of this long age (Matt. xxviii. 19, 20). From this fact alone we should be justified in assuming with absolute certainty that the directions needed for carrying out the command are to be found **upon the surface** of Scripture, and are there expressed in such manner as to be easily understood by those who have neither extraordinary intellects nor scholarly attainments. It is inconceivable that the needed information for doing a thing universally commanded to be done to every convert promptly upon his conversion, should be buried so deeply in the Word as to be accessible only to the profoundest scholars and comprehensible only to the subtlest intellects. No. The plain simple words which the Holy Spirit has used when speaking of **baptism itself** give all the needed information, and in such manner as to be easily understood by plain simple men. It could not be otherwise. Why should it be supposed that the directions concerning baptism are not to be sought in those Scriptures which speak of baptism, but are to be elucidated by processes of the intellect from supposed analogies to circumcision, or from conjectural meanings of Old Testament types and shadows?

If the plain words that speak of baptism, which tell us who were baptized and how it was done, were not intended to **lead** the unlearned servants of Christ (and He had none other at the start, Acts iv. 13) in carrying out the ministry committed to them, then they could only serve to **mis**lead; and this is inconceivable.

As to the "how" of baptism, the word itself contains full and definite information, for the English of the Greek word **baptizo** is **to immerse.** Had the Greek word been **translated** in our English versions, instead of **transliterated** we should have (as in Rotherham's version) the word "immerse" wherever we now read "baptize." The prevalence of the unscriptural and Romish practice of infant baptism at the time of the translation of the Bible into English accounts for the presence, in our English Bible, of the Greek word "baptize"; for by that word the meaning is hidden from English readers who are ignorant of Greek. If the Greek word **baptizo** had been treated by the translators in the same way as all other words of the Greek text were treated by them, that is to say, if an English word of equivalent meaning had been put in the English version to represent it, there would be no uncertainty in the minds of ordinary English readers as to how baptism is to be administered.

As to the persons who are to be baptized, clear directions are found, in a form understandable by the "ignorant and unlearned," in such words as "**He** that **believeth** and is baptized shall be saved"; "they that **gladly received his word** were baptized"; "when they **believed** . . . they were baptized"; "many Corinthians hearing, **believed** and were baptized".

These words clearly tell us that **believers** are baptized; and it is admitted on all hands that there is no command to baptize others than believers, and no recorded instance in Scripture of the baptism of any who were not believers.

It is surely safe to follow such plain directions as these, and surely is very unsafe to depart from them, giving heed to questionable analogies and far-fetched inferences.

In the minds of some readers the question will arise, Who should baptize? The idea that baptism is a "Sacrament," and that the authority to administer baptism is lodged with a self-perpetuating class of clergy, has its origin in Romish error, not in the Word of God.

It will be observed that, in all the Scriptures which speak of baptism, the stress is laid upon the act, and never on the person who does it. Manifestly no special qualification is necessary beyond that the baptizer should be a follower of Christ.

In John iv. 2 it is stated that "Jesus baptized not, but His disciples."

The charge to preach and to baptize was given by the Lord to His disciples without distinction (Matt. xxviii. 19).

Saul of Tarsus was baptized by "a certain disciple at Damascus named Ananias" (Act ix. 10). Paul refers to this disciple as being simply "one Ananias, a devout man according to the law" (Acts xxii. 12).

Paul himself baptized few of his converts, but left that to the disciples who accompanied him (1 Cor. i. 15, 16).

It is clear from these Scriptures that any disciple of

the Lord Jesus may baptize one who believes in Him. And this has evidently been appointed with a view to making it always possible for a convert to be baptized without delay. Clearly the Scriptures do not provide for a special class of disciples having the authority exclusively to administer baptism. That authority has been wrongfully usurped by a priestly class.

CONCLUSION

In view of the Scriptures that have been examined in this paper, the reader, if a believer who has not been baptized **as such,** is most earnestly urged not to risk the consequences of disobedience in a matter to which the Word of God attaches such great importance. And if it has chanced that, while he was yet an irresponsible infant, some one caused him to be sprinkled with water, or even put him under water, as a religious ceremony, he is urged not to rest upon an unauthorized, or what is at the best a very questionable, procedure, when simple obedience, with the certainty of being in accord with the Lord's will, is so easy. No prudent person would take such a risk, in like circumstances, even about a matter of temporal interest; and we are here speaking of that which involves eternal consequences.

These comments upon the great subject of Baptism, which we have shown to be closely connected with the foundation truths of Christianity, are earnestly commended to the prayerful attention of the people of God.

PART II

HOUSE HOLD BAPTISM

HOUSEHOLD BAPTISM

BY

PHILIP MAURO
Author of
"The World and its God," "The Number of Man,"
"Life in the Word," "Man's Day,"
"Reason to Revelation," etc.

INTRODUCTION

THE subject of baptism has occupied the writer's mind for a considerable period of time. It has been pressed upon his attention in a variety of ways; particularly through letters from esteemed correspondents asking his opinion as to the teaching of Scripture on that subject. In this way he was impelled to devote the time required for a special study of baptism, feeling that, in a matter of such importance, the Scripture must speak clearly. The conclusions reached have been set forth in the book entitled **Baptism: Its Place and Importance in Christianity**—to which these pages have now been added.

While in the midst of these studies, a beloved brother sent a copy of a paper, written by himself, in defence of "Household Baptism" (so called), and asked the writer's opinion of it. About the same time, from another source, came a copy of another pamphlet entitled **"The Symbols**

of Christ's Death", advocating "Household Baptism," with the request for an expression of opinion upon it. This called for further searching of the Scriptures to test the foundations of this special doctrine, the peculiar feature of which is that the believing head of a household should baptize his unbelieving children. (Consistent "Household Baptists" hold that unbelieving servants should also be baptized as members of the household.)

Although the number of those who hold this doctrine is not large, nevertheless, as an illustration of the remarkable contrariety of opinion about baptism, it is of interest and importance. Moreover, an examination of the grounds on which it is based will serve to throw further light upon the subject of baptism broadly. Therefore, we give here the letter written as a review of the paper in question, to which have been added some explanatory footnotes, and also a note at the end, giving the Scripture usage of the words "House" and "Household."

CHAPTER I

PART I

MY DEAR____,__I have carefully read, several times, your printed letter on the subject of "Household Baptism," have examined the Scriptures cited, and have studied the conclusion you have drawn from them. And now, at your request, I write to tell you what I think about it. As this discussion has to do with a **command of the Lord,** which all Christians are under obligation to obey, it is a matter of the first importance, and I shall endeavour to treat it accordingly.*

---

*The command is both to the disciples (and primarily to them) and also to believers. The disciples are commanded to baptize, and the converts to be baptized. But the obedience of disciples in baptizing may be assumed. They obey as Peter did at Pentecost, namely, by commanding those who received the Word to repent and be baptized. Therefore, we speak only of the command to the believer, with whom the decision really rests.

You will agree with me, I am sure, that we cannot be excused for misunderstanding a command which the Lord has given for our obedience. We cannot plead lack of clearness in His instructions; and hence, while it may be permissible to have differences of opinion as to details of prophecy, dispensational points, and the like, there should be no room for a difference in regard to the essential features of baptism.

I am glad to say I agree heartily with what you have written as to the **importance** of baptism, and in great part with what you say as to its significance. The Scriptures fully support you in saying that "baptism itself stands for something," "that baptism itself is in some way connected with salvation," that baptism, instead of merely standing for faith, "stands for **itself,** and means something which faith, from the very nature of things, cannot mean." We would both admit, of course, that baptism is **incidentally,** a testimony to others of the baptized one's faith in Christ; but most certainly that is not its **primary** signification. It is not merely a sign of something **already effected** through faith, but, as you well say, "the act of baptism itself effects something." It seems to me that one must read the Scriptures with closed eyes who does not see this; and I should be disposed to state the proposition even more strongly than you have done.

Regarding the special subject of your paper, it is to be regretted that the expression "Household Baptism" is used in this connection. There is, of course, no controversy as to baptizing a household when all its members have the Scriptural qualifications for baptism; though of necessity it is the **individual person,** each for himself, that is to be baptized. The only controversy arises over the question of baptizing **infants or other unconverted persons,** on the ground of the faith of the head of the house. Baptism is, beyond question, an **individual** and **personal** matter. It is the voluntary act of a responsible person. It is a rite which affects the standing of the person baptized, and none other. Hence, from the very nature of the case, such an expression as used by Paul in 1 Cor. i. 16, "I baptized also the household of Stephanas," and others like it, are merely convenient generalizations, specifying as a group the individual members of a household who had been baptized. Such convenient expression is used when the purpose of the Scripture does not require enumeration of the baptized individuals. Surely the strictly personal and individual character of baptism is in no wise affected by the references in the Scriptures to baptizing a household. It is written, for example, that Joshua circumcised "all the people" (Josh. v. 8), yet we know, of course, that only the males were circumcised.*

In order to secure a foundation for the practice of

---

*See note at end on Scripture usage of "House" and "Household."

baptizing the infant children of a believer, it is necessary to make two assumptions, both of which are wholly unwarranted; namely (1) that there were infants in the "household" of Stephanas at Corinth, and of Lydia and the Jailer respectively, at Philippi; and (2) that those infants were baptized along with the adult and believing members of those families. Only by doing great violence to the word "household" can we force it to yield that meaning. Especially is this to be reprobated when done for the purpose of obtaining a foundation for infant baptism, since it is perfectly obvious that those Scriptures were not given to teach or to sanction that practice. The expression is used only by Paul, and by Luke (his companion) in recording the ministry of Paul; and that was not until more than a quarter of a century after baptism became well known through the ministry of John the Baptist and the disciples of Christ. The practice of baptism was well settled long before the date of the first reference in the Bible to baptizing a household. Hence there is no warrant to found a doctrine on such expression.

The fact that Scripture records not a single case of the baptism of an infant is evidence of the **weightiest** kind, and should be accepted as **conclusive** by one who believes, as you and I do, that the silences and omissions of Scripture are just as much matters of Divine arrangement as its statements. The weight of this evidence is augmented by the statement in Acts viii. 12:

"But when they **believed** . . . they were baptized, **both men and women.**" No children are mentioned.* I press this earnestly upon you because the matter before us is one in regard to which it is a sin to err. And if, perchance, it be that I am the one who is in error, you will render me a great service in convincing me, by the Word of God, that such is the case.

I will now discuss the points made in your paper, but not in the precise order there found.

JOHN THE BAPTIST

Your reference to John's baptism is made for the purpose of deducing from it a principle that shall be broad enough to include the baptism of infants. You

---

*The writer of the paper we are reviewing thinks that the principle of baptism of children of believing parents was so well understood that the silence of Scripture is thereby fully accounted for. But inasmuch as the baptism of John was admittedly the first administration of that rite, and inasmuch as John admittedly baptized only responsible adults who confessed themselves to be sinners, it is clear that the omission of any subsequent reference in Scripture to the baptism of any infant or junior member of a family is a most weighty fact against the doctrine under discussion.

seem to think you have found such a principle in the circumstance that John warned certain who came to his baptism to bring forth "fruits meet for repentance." You say,

"He addresses those who come to him as 'a generation of vipers.' Yet he does not on this account refuse to baptize them; but he is very careful to tell them the responsibility that attaches to baptism, and that nothing less than fruits meet for repentance will suffice" (p. 4).

Now, had you turned at once to apply this action of the Baptist to the matter of infant baptism, you would have seen that it completely rules that practice out; for infants could not bring forth fruits meet for repentance, and could not assume any responsibility. But instead of applying the Scripture to the matter in hand, you seek to deduce from it the general principle that baptism is "with a view to the future," *i.e.* has a **future** aspect. You even say, "the great and overshadowing question in it all related to the future" (p. 5). Then, in utilizing this principle for the purpose of your argument, you say that John baptized "**in view of Christ's coming**"; and you ask, "Could anything be more clear as to the intent of baptism? On what possible ground, then, can there be an valid objection to children being baptized **in view of becoming Christians** and walking in newness of life?" (p. 25).* This is a very strange question. Because John baptized responsible **adults,** warning them, in view of

Christ's coming, you infer that it is proper to baptize **unconscious infants** in view of **something quite different.**† My comment is that, even if there were not already overwhelming scriptural evidence and reasons against the baptizing of infants, the facts you bring out in connection with John's baptism would suffice to shut it out of the pale of Christianity.

In the first place, your "principle" is not deducible from the recorded facts. Those who "went out" to John "were baptized of him in Jordan **confessing their sins**" (Matt. iii. 6). Thus, the first recorded words about John's baptism effectually exclude infants from that rite. It was for those who **confessed their sins.** And, in confirmation of this, we read, concerning John, that "all the people that **heard** him, and the publicans, **justified God,** being baptized with the baptism of John. But the Pharisees and lawyers **rejected the counsel of God against**

---

*The very form of this question contains the admission that there is no warrant in Scripture for infant baptism. All the writer can argue is that there is no "valid objection" to it.

†In connection with this argument of our friend, it should be noted that whereas John's baptism unto repentance was expressly in preparation for something which God had announced and which therefore was sure to happen, household baptists baptize their children in view only of a possibility.

themselves, being **not baptized** of him" (Luke vii. 29, 30).

John's baptism then, was for those who, admitting that God had a "counsel" against themselves, publicly confessed their sins, and thereby "justified God." Thus it clearly appears that John's baptism had primarily a **past aspect,** rather than a **future** aspect, and that infants and **other unrepentant persons had no part in it.**

The foregoing words are exceedingly important as bearing on the **doctrine** of baptism. According to the teaching of Romans, God justifies believing sinners, by His grace, through the redemption that is in Christ Jesus (Rom. iii. 21-26). But, in thus justifying the sinner, it is of the utmost importance that **God Himself** should be justified. **God's** righteousness is the important thing, and is mentioned four times in the passage last cited. Then the sinner whom God has justified is baptized. He thus justifies God in owning himself worthy of death. But God has **provided a death for him,** even the death of Jesus Christ. So we are taught the wondrous truth that "so many **of us** (justified sinners) **as were baptized into Jesus Christ** were baptized into His death" (Rom. vi. 3). To be baptized into **that** death is **salvation;** because it is the gateway into **Resurrection** (Ver. 5). As stated in Col. ii. 12: "Buried **with Him** in baptism, wherein **also** ye are **risen with Him,** through faith of the operation of God, who raised Him from the dead.

Thus it appears that Baptism is closely connected with Justification. It is for those whom God has justified; and it has a **Godward aspect,** for it justifies God in justifying sinners through the death and resurrection of Christ. It signifies, not merely that the sinner goes symbolically into the waters of death as his just due, but also, and chiefly, that he is baptized **not into his own death,** but into the death of **One who is risen from the dead.** The further we go into the subject the more impossible is infant baptism seen to be.

Moreover, the record shows that John baptized only such as responded, by the promptings of their own conscience, to his "preaching the baptism of repentance for the remission of sins" (Luke iii. 3). It was **only** for such as sought remission of their sins. As said in Luke vii. 39, "All the people **that heard him.**" This also excludes infants.

But, as already pointed out, the very words from which you deduce the **future** aspect of John's baptism are equally effectual to exclude infants. The admonitions to which you refer were spoken to soldiers, publicans, etc. Of course, there were no infants among these. Moreover, those admonitions could not have been spoken to infants, or heeded by them.

Therefore, what John's baptism teaches, as to the special point under consideration, is that baptism is for those **who consciously renounce, and wish to be rid of, the sins of their past life, and who purpose to live**

thereafter in a different manner.

Finally, the fact that John's ministry was preparatory to the coming of the Lord, and that he announced One mightier than himself who was to come after him, tells strongly **against,** and not in favour of, your proposition. That, which had a future aspect **then, lies in the past now.** In this respect John's baptism differs from Christian baptism. So that, in no conceivable view of the matter can the fact that John, before the Lord's coming, baptized responsible **adults** who came to him **confessing their sins,** in anticipation of One who was to come, afford the slightest pretext for baptizing **irresponsible infants,** or unrepentant persons, **after Christ has** come, and in view of something else.*

But even if the facts yielded the principle you endeavour to deduce therefrom, that principle would not suit your purpose, for the reason that it is **far too broad.** Manifestly, it affords just as much reason for baptizing the children of unconverted parents as those of converted parents. If it validates the baptism of **any** infants, it validates the baptism of **all.** For the children

---

*John's baptism was not the baptism of those who believed on the crucified and risen Christ, hence those who had received John's baptism had to be baptized again in the Name of the Lord before they could be recognized as Christians, and receive the Holy Ghost (Acts xix. 1-6).

of unbelieving parents have before them the possibility of becoming Christians. And inasmuch as you repudiate infant baptism, except in the special case of those having believing parents (or a believing parent), the principle you have been at such pains to deduce will not suit your purpose at all.

Evidently you realize, as all must, that, considering the place and importance given in the New Testament to John's baptism, infant baptism **must be found there, if it has God's sanction at all.** (The baptism of John was "from heaven"—Mark xi. 30; John i. 33.) In fact, it is not found there. John baptized no infants, but, on the contrary, the record we have of John's baptism effectually excludes infants from it. This in itself is quite enough to dispose of the whole question in the absence of any explicit command admitting infants to Christian baptism.*

---

*We would enter a general word of warning against the method by which our friend attempts to justify the practice for which he contends, namely, by deducing from one specific instance a so-called "principle," and then utilizing the latter to establish a specific instance quite different from that which supplied the "principle." By this method it is possible to make a given instance prove almost anything one pleases. All that is necessary is to make the "principle" broad enough to cover **both** instances,—the given instance and the desired

THE TRUE SIGNIFICANCE OF BAPTISM

You attempt to find in the Scriptures that tell us the significance of baptism, an argument in support of baptizing the unconverted children of a believer. And you lay it down as a proposition that we should first ascertain the **meaning** of the rite, and from that deduce how it should be carried out. But I submit that this is an error in method. When the Lord gives us something to

---

one,—and the result will be attained. It is not putting the matter too strongly to say that results attained by this method are utterly worthless. It is a fallacy (familiar to students of logic) whereby it is sought to establish a desired conclusion from a given fact by the simple process of introducing a middle term (in this case the so-called "principle") which is broad enough to include both the premise and the desired conclusion. It should be obvious that John's baptizing in view of the Coming of Christ furnishes no reason whatever why children should be baptized in view of their (possibly) growing up and being converted. It would just as readily prove that anybody might be baptized in view of anything else that might possibly happen thereafter. For surely, if the method be sound, one might argue that since John's baptism looked to the future, therefore every one should be baptized who looked to the future, regardless of what he was looking for.

do, our part is to do it without delay, and without inquiry as to His reasons for commanding it. We can study into the spiritual significance of it **afterwards.** In the case of baptism the **practice** preceded the explanation of the **doctrine** by many years. The Lord's commands, given when about to part from His disciples, are, and **must be,** sufficient **by themselves** for the proper fulfilment of those commands. If we look to His words we find in them no room whatever for infant baptism; and it is altogether a wrong mode of procedure to form a theory as to the significance of baptism from study of the Epistles, written long after, and then try to fit that theory into the Lord's words.

You probably would agree that the Israelites did not understand the spiritual significance of the rite of circumcision, or of the offerings. Yet they had no difficulty in **doing** the things commanded.

In carrying out this line of argument you contrast on page 6 two "conceptions" of baptism, one being that which you attribute to the "Baptists," and the other that which you hold yourself. I quote—

"To Baptists baptism is simply a looking back (something already true of the believer is represented by an outward sign). To John it was a looking forward."

You further say—

"Baptists limit the thought of obedience to the act itself. John made it a committal to a lifelong obedience."

And you ask, "Which of these conceptions is the correct one?" To that question I should unhesitatingly answer, "Neither." If any Baptists hold that baptism is merely a sign of something that has been **already effected** through the act of believing in Christ, they certainly do greatly err. I have already expressed my concurrence in your view that baptism itself effects something—and I will add that it effects "something" that is of great importance. Moreover, what baptism effects is something which **could not possibly be effected for an unconverted person.** So that what you bring out touching the importance of baptism furnishes another conclusive reason against infant baptism. This I will seek to establish more clearly later on.

In saying that "John made it (baptism) a committal to a lifelong obedience" you make use of a vague expression, whose very vagueness provides a loophole for infant baptism to slip in. If you will just call to mind that **not John,** but those who were baptized **themselves** made all the "committal" that was made, and will further try to imagine how John could possibly have made the baptism of infants the "committal" of such infants "to a lifelong obedience," you will see that you cannot, by means of this contrast of supposed "conceptions" of baptism, lay any support for the practice of baptizing unconverted or unrepentant persons.

It seems to me that the very method you adopt in trying to find support for infant baptism furnishes a strong case against it.

You next refer to Mark xvi. 16: **"He that believeth and is baptized shall be saved."**

Certainly these words do clearly prove, as you say, that "Baptism itself is in some way connected with Salvation"; and further prove that for a man "to be saved **in the sense meant here,** he must not only believe, but be baptized." Those words of the Lord are indeed so clear as to leave no room for any inquiry as to their meaning, except only as to "the sense meant here" by the word "saved." Into that, however, there is now no need to inquire; for certainly there is **no sense at all** in which an infant can be "saved" by being baptized. Or, if that be too positive a statement, I will put it this way; I know of no scriptural usage of the word "salvation" which would describe what a baptized infant comes into; and your paper refers to none.

But, in your argument with the "Baptists" you insist, and very properly, that we must follow the **precise order** of the Lord's words. Do you not see, then, that the order is "**Believe** and be **baptized**"? that the **believing** precedes the being baptized? You object that the "Baptists" virtually make these words read: "He that believeth and **is saved** shall be baptized." But by no possibility can the words be applied to infants unless made to read, "He that is baptized (provided he has a believing parent) and believes after he grows up shall be saved." If any words can restrict baptism in such a way as to exclude infants without naming them, those words of the Lord Jesus certainly do. And I put it to your enlightened conscience that it is just as wrong to broaden the Lord's words as to narrow them. "He that believeth" defines with absolute precision the necessary qualification for baptism.

But that is not all. The preceding verse contains an essential part of the command. "Go ye into all the world, and preach the gospel to every creature. He that believeth and is baptized shall be saved." So it is **believing the Gospel** that qualifies one for baptism; and the Gospel is the remission of sins through the blood of Christ to all who repent and believe in Him. Manifestly infants cannot hear the Gospel and cannot repent or believe.

Finally, the words "and is baptized" imply the **voluntary** act of the one for whom the command is intended.

Acts ii. 38: "Repent, and be baptized every one of you in the Name of the Lord Jesus for the remission of your sins." It needs but a moment's reflection to see that these words exclude those who can neither hear nor repent. The absence of any command to those believing on the Lord (they were Jews "out of every nation under heaven," ver. 5) to baptize their children on returning home, is a telling fact against the modern theory of "household baptism."

Acts xxii. 16. Ananias to Saul, "Arise, and be baptized, and wash away thy sins."

You rightly reject the explanation given by some that this expression "wash away thy sins" applied only to the special case of Saul of Tarsus. The plain meaning of the words is as you say, namely that, "It was evidently a water baptism, and it was a washing away of sins." If, then, this was not a **special** baptism, but just the **common Christian baptism** (as you rightly say), do you not see how fatal this passage is to infant baptism? Did you say to your own infants, "Arise, and be baptized, and wash away thy sins, calling on the Name of the Lord"? Could you say that to any infant? Could any infant meet those conditions? Manifestly not. If baptism is a washing away of one's sins, then most certainly infants cannot be baptized.

The explanation given in your paper of the words "wash away thy sins" does not bear directly on the question before us. You say that the Apostle's sins "were gone from **before God.** This was a washing away from **before men.**" (black type mine). But what warrant have you for saying that Saul's sins were gone "from before God"? And how could they be gone from before God and yet exist on him before men? If already gone from before God, how could they be washed away? Are not the words "before men" an unauthorized interpolation; and do they not manifestly destroy the sense of the passage? And before what men did Paul wash away his sins? I know of no Scripture that makes baptism necessarily a public matter. I know we are warranted by the Scriptures in saying that Paul's sins were **pardoned,** by God's grace, when he believed on the Lord Jesus. But "wash away" conveys a further thought. Inasmuch as **God** had pardoned them, it was possible for **Paul** to wash them away, and be clean every whit. In this connection I would remind you that baptism is "the demand of a good conscience **toward God**" (1 Pet. iii. 21). Baptism is **demanded** of one who has, because of the pardon of his sins, obtained "a good conscience." God Himself demands it; and the one whose conscience has been purged should demand it too. And it is "toward God," not toward men.

Peter tells us explicitly that baptism is not a mere washing of the surface of the body (a "putting away of the filth of the flesh"), but it has to do with the **conscience.** And all this merely makes infant baptism more and more of an impossibility.

Rom. vi. 3, 4: "So many of us as were baptized unto Jesus Christ, were baptized unto His death," etc.

I am in agreement with you that, according to this Scripture, "one who has not been baptized could not say he had been buried with Christ." It follows that an infant could not possibly be baptized. Moreover, the door to infant baptism is fully closed by the words, "So many **of us** as were baptized." The words "of us" limit the statement to the saints. Furthermore, the immediate context limits it to such as could ask the question, "Shall we continue in sin?"

That these words were chosen with intent is proved by Gal. iii. 27: "For as many **of you** as have been **baptized into Christ** have put on Christ." The meaning of the words "of you" is fixed with absolute certainty by the preceding verse: "For ye are all **the children of God by faith in Christ Jesus.**" It follows that none but "children of God," such as have been born from above, can, by means of baptism, "put on Christ." The Scripture absolutely shuts out the baptism of infants and other unconverted persons.

THE CROSSING OF THE RED SEA

I Cor. x. 1, 2. This Scripture is referred to at many points in your paper and calls for special notice. Of it you say—

"Speaking of Israel as a nation Paul says they were all baptized unto Moses in the cloud and in the sea (p. 11).

"The passage of the Red Sea is said to be the baptizing of all Israel unto Moses. *Yet this included children* (italics yours, p. 20).

"The fact remains that they (children) were baptized, and it is no less person than St. Paul, the special minister of the Church, who tells us so (p. 20).

"If children were baptized at the Red Sea they can be baptized to-day, for the Apostle does not intimate any change in the rite or its application (p. 21).

"Children as well as grown people could be separated by baptism from Egypt at the Red Sea" (p. 27).

"Nothing you can say can alter the fact that actual children were baptized at the Red Sea" (p. 30).

So you evidently build much upon this Scripture, and it is of special importance because it is the **only** Scripture in which you claim to find the practice of infant baptism.

I greatly marvel, therefore, that in none of the numerous references you make to this Scripture do you quote the inspired words that tell **who were baptized at the Red Sea.** You say that Paul, "speaking of **Israel as a nation**" says that "they were all baptized unto Moses." And again you declare that the passage of the Red Sea "is said to be the baptizing of **all Israel** unto Moses," and you add in italic type, **"Yet this included children."** And you boldly state that "nothing you can say can alter the fact that **actual children** were baptized at the Red Sea."

Does the Apostle Paul, or rather does the Spirit of God, who was speaking by him, so say? And could you have based your argument upon the **actual words which the Spirit used**? No. The inspired words afford no footing whatever for infant baptism. On the contrary, there are evidences in this Scripture of very special care to avoid giving any possible standing ground for that doctrine. What the Apostle says is— "that ALL OUR

FATHERS were under the cloud, and all passed through the sea, and were **all baptized** unto Moses in the cloud and in the sea."*

How careful the Spirit of God has been to use no terms here which could give countenance to infant baptism! The words even distinguish between **passing through the sea,** and **being baptized.** The "fathers" all passed through the sea, **and** were **also "baptized unto Moses."** You, in every case, not only substitute "all Israel" for "fathers," and actually state that this "included children," but you make the crossing of the sea to be the baptism. It is very significant indeed that, while the children passed through the sea (though no mention is made of the fact) only the "fathers" were "baptized unto Moses." So infants may now be passed through water, but that act would not be **baptism.**

Thus, even if the crossing of the Red Sea had been a

---

*An attempt has been made to avoid the crushing effect of this Scripture by saying that the words "all our fathers" might be taken to include those who were infants at the time, and who afterwards became "fathers" (unless they became **mothers**). But there is no escape in this direction, for the Scripture goes on to say that "some of them," the fathers who were baptized, committed the idolatry of the Golden Calf, and the other wicked acts mentioned. The meaning, therefore, is fixed beyond the shadow of a doubt.

"rite," as you say, though it was not that, but merely an incident of the journey of the Israelites, the inspired account of it nevertheless absolutely excludes infants from "the baptism unto Moses." The "fathers" only were baptized unto that leader.*

---

*From this Scripture we can learn with certainty that baptism is for those who have responsibility for their actions. This is why the Spirit of God makes the baptism unto Moses something distinct from the passage of the sea. The infants, the mixed multitude, the flocks and herds all crossed the sea, but to **the fathers only** was it a baptism. This Scripture affords just as much ground for the baptism of cattle and household goods as for the baptism of infants. If the arguments of our friends proved anything it would be that the parents' obedience in the matter of baptism availed the child, so far as any faithfulness of the parent could avail it. For the principle for which our friends contend is that the Lord includes the household in blessings bestowed on the head of the house for faith and obedience on his part. This principle, so far as it applies (and it would be easy to stretch it too far) really furnishes an additional argument against the baptism of unconverted members of a household. Thus, in 1 Cor. vii. 13-14, we read that the unbelieving husband is sanctified by the (believing) wife, and the unbelieving wife is sanctified by the (believing) husband. That is to say, the unbelieving one is sanctified for the purpose of

And then let us note carefully what follows. "With many **of them** (the baptized ones, the fathers, **not the children**) God was not well pleased; for they—the fathers, **not the children**—were overthrown in the wilderness." They (the fathers, who had been responsibly "baptized unto Moses") provoked God in many ways. They committed idolatry, they committed fornication, etc. The whole point of the passage is the warning conveyed by what happened to those responsible "fathers" who had been consciously "baptized unto Moses," whereof the children knew nothing. If the infants took part in the baptism, they took part in the other things also; for the **same persons** form the subject of the entire passage. But, as we know, the little ones were kept alive, and were brought into the land, **though they were not baptized.** It was the **baptized**

---

the marriage relation with the believing one, otherwise conjugal relations could not be lawfully maintained. And the Apostle adds, "else were your children unclean; but now are they holy" (*i.e.* sanctified, so that association with them in the family relationship is proper). How clear it is that the unbelieving members of the family are "sanctified," not because they have been baptized, which is not so much as hinted at, but because of the faith of the husband or wife! So this Scripture also seems to contain an implied prohibition of baptism for the unbelieving members of the household.

ones only that were shut out. As God said immediately after the "provocation," "But your **little ones,** which ye said should be a prey, **them will I bring in,** and they shall know the land which ye have despised" (Num. xiv. 31).

Here is, indeed, a solemn lesson for baptized believers of to-day. But not many will even listen to it. There is much profitable warning in 1 Cor. x. (and in Heb. iii. and iv., where the same incidents are referred to), which are expressly written for the responsible saints of this dispensation; for all these things were written for **our** admonition, who have been baptized into the death and resurrection of Christ. But there is no ground given here for infant baptism.

THE ARK OF NOAH

You point out that Noah and his children were all saved in the ark, and that this was on the ground of Noah's faith, with not a word said, either in the Old Testament or the New, as to the faith of his sons. I am sure you would not maintain that any children are **saved** by the faith of their parents, and without faith on their part. This is what your argument would prove, if it proved anything. But the reference to Noah will not support your proposition. Noah's children were grown married men, responsible for their own actions. The fact that they went into the ark showed their faith. In this they differed from Lot's sons-in-law who remained in Sodom and perished.

It is a striking fact indeed, seeing that the ark is likened in 1 Pet. iii. 20, 21 to baptism, that there were no infants in it. Extraordinary indeed is the care which the Spirit of God has taken to close every door against the intrusion of a doctrine from which, nevertheless, the people of God have suffered most grievously.

The several cases to which you refer—Abraham and his house, Noah and his house, a lamb for a house—might conceivably be used to support the proposition that the children of godly parents will be **saved.** But you use them to prove that the children of believing parents should be **baptized.** To **that** proposition they lend no support at all, but quite the reverse.*

CIRCUMCISION

You next attempt to find in the practice of circumcision a reason for baptizing infants. You say, "If

---

*If the parent's **faith** avails anything to his child, then, by analogy, the parent's baptism might avail the child in some way; but the idea that baptism, apart from the faith of the one baptized, avails anything, is plainly contrary to Scripture.

circumcision applied to children of eight days old even, why should not baptism?" I am surprised that you should ask such a question, and am more surprised that, in your discussion of circumcision, you wholly omit to give the reason why children were circumcised on the eighth day. The simple reason is that **God commanded** that "he that is **eight days old** shall be circumcised among you, every man child in your generations" (Gen. xvii. 12). God strictly defined those who were to be circumcised, and fixed the time when it was to be done, namely, a few (eight) days after their birth. God has also strictly defined those who are to be baptized, namely, those who believe the Gospel; and while no law is given as to the precise day when it is to be done, the Scriptures clearly indicate that it should be promptly after believing.* Circumcision was explicitly for male infants, and for them only. Baptism is just as explicitly for believing sinners, male and female. Circumcision was for the children of Abraham, **all** of them, "every male child." Baptism is for the children of God, **all** of them, without distinction of sex. For in Christ there is neither male or female.

The analogy between circumcision and baptism is

---

*It is sufficient to cite the immediate baptism of those who on the day of Pentecost received the Word: that of the Eunuch by Philip; and that of the Philippian jailer and his household. There was no delay in any case.

plain. Infants were eligible for the former because every one of the children of Israel was, by his natural birth, within the terms of God's promises to Abraham, Isaac, and Jacob. No work of God **in** an Israelite was needed to make him one of the natural seed of Abraham. Natural birth made him an Israelite, and hence a proper subject for circumcision. But, to bring a sinner within the scope of the **new** covenant, ratified in the blood of Christ, a work of God in the heart **is** needed. He must be born from above; and then immediately, **but not before,** can he be "buried with Christ" in baptism, and assume to "walk in newness of life." Spiritual birth is required to make any individual a proper subject for baptism. The analogy is so plain I wonder that any can fail to see it.

"AN OUTWARD SPHERE OF PRIVILEGE"

I come now to a feature of the doctrine of "Household Baptism," against which I must raise a strong protest. You say that—"Baptism introduces into outward relationship with God, and into a sphere of outward privilege" (p. 20). Again, "But if there is an outward place of privilege, and the entry to it is by the rite of baptism, then the passage (Rom. xi.) becomes clear at once. From such privilege **mere** professors may be 'cut off' " (p. 29).

You must permit me to say that the idea that God

sanctions a sphere of mere profession, and that the solemn rite of baptism was appointed to admit persons—converted persons and unconscious infants alike—to that sphere, is to me simply shocking. Here lies the chief ground of my objection to "household baptism," so called. And it gives me real pain to find the sevenfold unity of the Spirit of Eph. iv. 4-6 broken up by human ingenuity into three "circles of privilege," in order to make a sphere of mere "profession," into which admission is had by baptism. Can you really mean what you say on p. 12, last paragraph, that the words of Eph. iv. 5, "one Lord, one faith, one baptism," define a sphere of profession? I do not know how to characterize this; so will only say that it distresses me to know that you can entertain such a view as this. "A **recognized** outward sphere of profession"—recognized, of course, **by God**—and they who are "buried with Him (Christ) by baptism," and raised with Him therein, and who thereby put on Christ, are merely brought by baptism into this "sphere of profession"!* What a distressing doctrine!

---

*In the paper we are reviewing, this sphere is not spoken of as one of **mere** profession, though it is distinctly said that "**mere** professors" are admitted to that sphere by baptism. But we, on the contrary, maintain that, in this era, God countenances **no** dead works of any sort, and the idea of administering the holy rite of baptism to one who is dead in sins is repugnant to

And how is this extraordinary idea supported? You tell us (p. 11) that the **Israelites** were "all baptized unto Moses" (though the Scripture says it was the **"fathers"** that were baptized); and then follows the assertion that their baptism meant "that they **professedly** accepted the guidance of the cloud, and that they had left Egypt for ever." By inserting here (and without the slightest warrant for so doing, but indeed in direct contradiction of the plainest facts) the word "professedly," it is sought to supply an argument for the doctrine of a recognized sphere of "profession" in God's dealings with men in this age.

All this was made to hang by the thread of the supposition that infants were put through the "rite" of baptism at the Red Sea; and I need say no more on that point. But here we have yet another idea interpolated, namely, that the "baptism" at the Red Sea brought the Israelites into a sphere of mere "profession." I do not see how anything could possibly be wider of the mark. The exodus from Egypt was a **real** exodus, not a sham. The crossing of the Red Sea was a **reality** for **every**

---

the very foundation principles of Christianity. Moreover, there is no such thing as a "recognized sphere of profession." The word translated "profession" should, in all its occurrences (1 Tim. vi. 12 and 13; Heb. iii. 4, 14, x. 23), read **con**-fession. That is a very different thing from **pro**-fession.

Israelite—children included (though it was a "baptism" only to the "fathers"). It was not a mere "profession." It brought them, **every one of them,** into a **real** wilderness, where they had **real** wilderness experiences, all of them. **There was not a "mere professor" in the entire company,** nor could there be. And what was real to them **physically,** is real to the baptized believer in Christ **spiritually.** He is redeemed by the "precious blood of Christ," and by baptism he is "buried with Christ," and also "**raised with Him,** through faith of the operation of God, who raised Him from the dead." Thus he passes out of the moral Egypt—this evil world—and enters upon a wilderness journey to walk with Christ "in newness of life." **No "mere professor" can possibly have any of these experiences.** None but a believer in the Lord Jesus Christ, none but a pardoned sinner, is eligible for baptism. That is as certain as Scripture can make it, by direct command, by practice, by type, and by doctrine.

Moreover, the baptized believer is solemnly warned, by the example of the baptized Israelites, not to lust after evil things as they also lusted, etc. For the warnings of 1 Cor. x. 1-12 are for Christians, not for "mere professors." The words are "that **we** should not lust"; "neither be **ye** idolators"; "neither murmur **ye,**" etc. Unconverted persons do not need those exhortations. What they need first is to repent and believe the Gospel.

If then there is, or could be, any "recognized sphere of

profession," most assuredly the crossing of the Red Sea is not the place to look for the type of it. That type forbids any recognized sphere of profession.

It seems to me, therefore, that after having started out to make much of baptism, you end by making nothing of it, and less than nothing. For surely no Divinely appointed gateway is needed to admit unconverted persons to the sphere of mere "profession." How can you possibly entertain the idea that Christ appointed baptism as the entrance to a sphere of profession, when He said distinctly, "He that believeth and is baptized shall be **saved**"?

You term this a "sphere of outward **privilege**." But what are the "privileges" to which infants who are sprinkled or immersed are admitted, or that mere professors enjoy? I have looked carefully through your paper to ascertain this, and can find nothing beyond the rather vague suggestion that baptized infants are entitled, when they grow up, to receive instruction in the Bible. But you do not show how baptism confers that privilege; and certainly it is not among the results effected by baptism according to Scripture, such as putting on Christ. Nor do I see why children who have not been baptized may not receive instruction in the Scriptures. I know of many who do. Christian parents are commanded to bring up their children in the fear and admonition of the Lord; and many directions are given to parents concerning their children. But they are not told to baptize them. That, most certainly, is excluded.

Nor do I find in your tract a reference to any Scripture telling what privileges God has appointed in this age for "mere professors." I have supposed it to be a cardinal principle of your teaching that now, since **the Man Jesus Christ is risen from the dead,** none have **any** standing before God save those who are "in Christ." None others are "recognized," whatever they may **profess.**

It is with these tremendous truths of Redemption that the Scriptures, not by one passage, but by many, link baptism. Therefore, I say, it causes pain and distress to read such statements as that there is an outward place of privilege, and the entry to it is by the rite of baptism. That the solemn rite appointed by our Lord, and which pertains to His own Death and Resurrection, should be degraded to this! How distressing!

It is because of the high character of the truth involved that I have gone so exhaustively into the whole subject, and have taken much pains in studying your paper, and in testing its various arguments by the Scriptures. Will you then do the same by this letter? This is not a matter of ordinary controversy. I am not merely setting up **my** view of a debatable point of doctrine against **yours.** There is too much at stake to let pride of opinion, or the fact that you are publicly committed to the doctrine of "household baptism," hinder you in giving **unbiased** consideration to what is herein placed before you. It will be evident to you that I do not write in a controversial spirit.

This letter is transmitted after much prayer, and in the earnest hope that, after pondering these things, you will put aside this wrong doctrine, and will be in accord with your brethren, to whom it is such a serious stumbling-block.

Ever sincerely yours in Christ.

www.ingramcontent.com/pod-product-compliance
Lightning Source LLC
Chambersburg PA
CBHW071054090426
42737CB00013B/2355